Active Database Systems:
Concept, Design and Applications

Dr.S. Meenakshi,

Associate Professor,

Department of Computer Science,

Gobi Arts & Science College, Gobichettipalayam.

Dr.V. Thiagarasu,

Associate Professor,

Department of Computer Science,

Gobi Arts & Science College, Gobichettipalayam.

Published by

Active Database Systems: Concept, Design and Applications

ISBN 978-93-86638-00-7

Authors

Dr.S. Meenakshi

Dr.V. Thiagarasu

Bonfring

309, 2nd Floor, 5th Street Extension, Gandhipuram,

Coimbatore-641 012.

Tamilnadu, India.

E-mail: info@bonfring.org

Website: www.bonfring.org

Phone: 0422 4213231

Preface

Database systems are the essential components of information system technology for storing and managing data and allow multiple users to access and manipulate data in a consistent and secured manner. A database system is a collection of databases and a database management system, which is effectively used to manage the data to meet the informational needs of any user or applications. Today database technology plays a major role in all areas where computers are used, including engineering, medicine, business, education and electronic commerce.

The technological advancements and growing global competitions in the computer hardware and software systems have influenced many changes in the development of database systems. More specifically, to create and manage data for efficient decision making, one should emphasis on the development of an advanced database management system, which organizes the data in an excellent manner. In order to satisfy the requirements of advanced applications, the field of database systems is aimed at increasing the functionality and performance of database systems. In the recent past, one of the advanced database system namely active database system, provides active mechanism to monitor the changes in database state and initiate appropriate actions automatically without user intervention, which is important for many advanced applications. In the active database system, the active behavior is incorporated using event-condition-action (ECA) rules paradigm.

This text book is written for anyone who wants to learn the basic concepts, data models, architecture, applications and various types of database systems in a simple way. The focus of this book is to present the concept, model, architecture and applications of active database systems. Also this book specifically describes the model, design and implementation issues of the active object-relational database system.

Organisation of the Book

This book is organized into the following chapters.

Chapter 1 discusses the basic concepts of database systems which include the definition, components of database manager, benefits and characteristics of database systems. This chapter explains the characteristics and classification of the database management system. Also this chapter describes the different categories of users in database systems. Finally this chapter presents the applications of database systems.

Chapter 2 deals with various data models, database system architecture, database development and database design. A clear understanding of data models is essential to organize the data in a specified structure for quick access and efficient management. This chapter explains the various data models which includes conceptual, representational and physical data models. This chapter describes the Entity-Relationship (ER) model which is the most popular high-level conceptual data model. This chapter explains the three important representational data models such as relational, object-oriented and object-relational data models. Physical data models describe how data is stored as files in the computer by representing information such as record formats, record orderings and access paths.

Also this chapter provides the concept of database system architecture. This chapter describes the two different architectural approaches for DBMS such as structure of a DBMS that provides various components to perform functions to its users and ANSI three-level architecture which includes the external, conceptual and internal levels to provide three different views of the data in database. Also this chapter presents client/server architecture which is the most common and flexible architecture that is used to implement multiuser database management system. This chapter describes the concept of database schema, database state and data independence.

Chapter 3 presents the various processes required for designing and developing a database. The database is an important component of an organization's information system. This chapter presents the various stages of the database development lifecycle. Database design is one of the important stages in database system lifecycle and a well defined database design is an essential process to meet the requirements of the organization. This chapter discusses the three important phases of database design which include conceptual, logical and physical database design.

The database systems are essential to define the constructs and formalisms to design and develop databases based on the requirements of database applications. This chapter presents an overview of three conventional database systems such as relational, object-oriented and object-relational database systems.

Chapter 4 explains the transaction management for managing the execution of transactions in a database system. This chapter presents the transaction concept which includes transaction states, transaction execution and transaction classification. The main goal of transaction management is to guarantee the correctness of the database state. When a database is shared and updated by multiple transactions concurrently, a correctness criterion is needed to ensure the correctness of the database. This chapter discusses the various correctness criteria such as serializability and non-serializability for defining the correctness of transaction execution in database systems. In general, serializability is the most widely accepted correctness criterion for controlling the order of concurrent execution of transactions and it is achieved through various concurrency control algorithms.

This chapter explains the various concurrency control algorithms to ensure the correctness for processing concurrent transactions in the database system. The three basic generic techniques used to design the concurrency control algorithms are locking, time-stamp ordering (pessimistic) and optimistic. This chapter also discusses the various types of transaction models used for transaction processing in database systems. A transaction model is basically a set of rules which governs the execution and properties of transactions.

Chapter 5 discusses the concept of active database systems. Active database systems provide active mechanism for monitoring the changes in database state and initiating appropriate actions automatically without user intervention which is important for multi-user database system. The active database system supports a number of features including integrity constraint enforcement, derived data maintenance, implementation of triggers and alerters, protection and version control, gather statistics for query optimization. The development of an active database system is carried out in two ways. One approach is to develop the entire database system from scratch. However this approach leads to a costlier one in terms of hardware and software. The other approach is, to embed the active database system into the existing database systems.

This chapter presents the need for active mechanism in databases systems. Also this chapter explains the functions of the active database system that include the specification and processing of active rules. This chapter describes the rule execution model of the active database system with its various phases. This chapter also presents the several issues for developing rule execution model of the active database system. Also this chapter specifies about active information system. This chapter discusses the abstract architecture and implementation of the active database system. The two types of architecture identified for implementing the active database system into the existing database systems are, layered and integrated architectures. The active database system is implemented in commercial database systems in a limited form of triggers. Finally this chapter presents the applications of the active database system in various domains.

Chapter 6 discusses the concept of active object-relational database systems. This chapter explains the knowledge and execution model of SQL3 standard for trigger definition and processing. This chapter presents the features of triggers in SQL3 standard and also in commercial database systems. This chapter describes the classification and the use of triggers in database systems. This chapter also illustrates the use of triggers in the object-relational database system using Oracle triggers. In the end, this chapter discusses the various issues related to the design and implementation of generic active rule system in active object-relational database system.

We sincerely hope that the content of this book will be useful to all learners of database management systems. Any constructive suggestion for further improvement of this book is most welcome.

Dr.S. Meenakshi
Dr.V. Thiagarasu

Acknowledgement

It is a great pleasure to acknowledge the support we received from various sources for writing this book.

First, we would like to thank the Almighty for His blessings to bring this book in a successful manner.

We would like to express our sincere thanks to the President, Secretary & Correspondent, Principal and colleagues of Gobi Arts & Science College for their encouragement and moral support for writing this book.

We express our special thanks to the family members for their support and encouragement for publishing this book.

We thank the publishers for their efforts to publish this book in a good and complete shape.

We also acknowledge the authors and researchers of database systems whose work has helped us in enhancing our knowledge on the subject for developing this book.

Dr.S. Meenakshi
Dr.V. Thiagarasu

<table>
<tr><th>Chapter</th><th style="text-align:center">Contents</th><th>Page No</th></tr>
</table>

CHAPTER-1

INTRODUCTION TO DATABASE SYSTEMS

Key Features

- Basics of Database Systems
- Need for Database Systems
- Characteristics of the DBMS
- Classification of DBMS
- Categories of Users in Database Systems
- Applications of Database Systems

1.1. Introduction

Database systems are the vital part of information system technology and they provide effective mechanism for storing and managing large volumes of data in a multiuser environment. Database system research and development is aimed at increasing the functionality and performance of database systems to accommodate the requirements of modern database applications. The main objectives of developing a database system include an efficient, flexible, reliable and secure management of data.

To learn the aspects of database technology, first understanding the basic concepts of database systems is essential. This chapter explains the basic concepts of database systems which include the definition, components of database manager, benefits and characteristics of database systems. This chapter presents the characteristics and classification of the DBMS. Also this chapter describes the different types of people involved in the database system environment. Finally this chapter presents the use of database systems in various application domains.

1.2. Basics of Database Systems

Database systems are become essential for managing huge amount of data to meet the informational needs of any user. A database system is a database management system together with one or more databases. A database is a collection of interrelated data stored together in a structured form that can be used by different users. The four elements of a database are:

- **Data** is a single piece of information. A multiple number of data elements in terms of field value can be stored in the form of a record in a database. A set of records again forms a file, which is then stored in the storage. For example information of a student in a student management system can be stored as a record with multiple field values, such as student register number, student name, department and marks.

- **Relationships** specify a mapping of association between various data elements.
- **Constraints** are used to define the correctness of the data in the database.
- **Schema** describes the organization of data and relationships within the database.

A database management system (DBMS) is a software system that enables the user to define, store, modify and access the data from a database in a consistent and secured manner. Defining a database involves specifying the data types, structures and constraints of the data to be stored in the database. Storing is the process of storing the data in the database using the storage medium. Modifying a database reflects changes in the data while performing the database operations such as insert, update and delete. Accessing a database involves the querying the database to retrieve the specific data that are already stored. The three important features of the DBMS are: persistency – if a program modifies certain data, the changes remain even after the program has terminated; sharing – more than one user or program can concurrently access the data; and reliability – the data must remain correct despite the hardware and software failures.

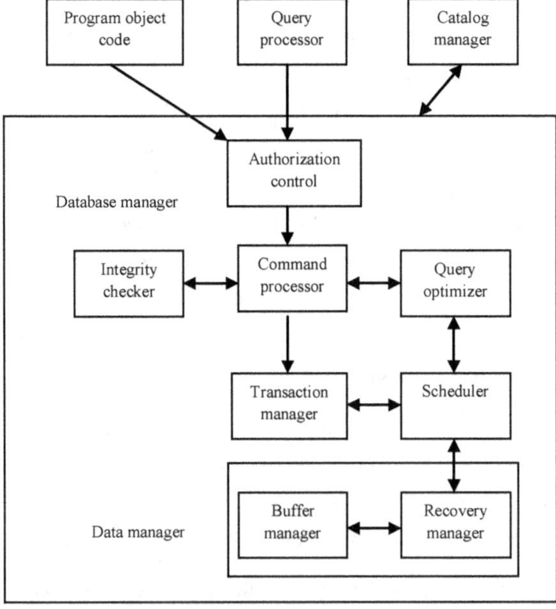

Figure 1.1: Components of Database Manager

Typically, a DBMS provides the various facilities such as Data Definition Language (DDL), Data Manipulation Language (DML) and several mechanisms for controlled access of database. DDL allows users to define the database, specify the data types, data structures and the constraints on the data to be stored in the database and it also translates the schema written in a source language into the object schema. DML allows users to insert, update, delete and retrieve data from the database and it also provides general query facilities through query language. The DBMS provides mechanism (software) for controlled access to the database such as security system for preventing unauthorized user trying to access the database, concurrency control system to allow shared access of the database and recovery system to a database to restore a previous consistent state because of hardware or software failures.

The DBMS is complex and sophisticated pieces of software that aims to provide the types of functions and services include data storage, retrieval and update, a user-accessible catalog, transaction support, concurrency control services, recovery services, authorization services support for data communication, integrity services, services to promote data independence and utility services. In order to provide these services, the DBMS should be designed with the different interrelated components such as database manager, query processor, file manager, DML processor, DDL processor and catalog manager.

Database manager is the central software component of the DBMS which interfaces with user submitted application programs and queries. The database manager is also called as database control system and it handles database access at runtime with the subcomponents such as authorization control, command processor, integrity checker, query optimizer, transaction manager, scheduler, recovery manager and buffer manager. The various components of the database manager are shown in Figure 1.1.

The database system consists of many components which defines and regulates the management and use of data within a database system environment. The various components of a database system environment are the following.

- Hardware – Computers, input/output devices and network components.
- Software – Operating system, database management system, application programs and utility programs.
- Data – Databases that describe the data used by the organization
- Procedures – Instructions and business rules that are to be applied for designing and use of the database systems.
- People – System administrator, database administrator, database designer, analyst, programmer and end-users.

The database systems provide information to meet the operational need as well as future planning for any organization. The implementation of a database system depends on the size, function and requirements of the organization.

1.3. Need for Database Systems

Before the introduction of a database system, data is stored and organized in the form of flies called as file based system. File based system focuses on the data processing needs of individual departments in the organization, instead of regarding the enterprise as a whole. The programmer responses to user requests by developing computer programs for individual application programs such as pay roll, accounts and inventory control. Each application program is designed with its own set of data files and each file has its own file management and processing. The advantages of the file based system are simplicity and customization. However its disadvantages are data redundancy, data inconsistency, limited data sharing and data dependence. Thus the database systems are essential to avoid the drawbacks of the file based system to organize and maintain the data.

A number of characteristics that differentiate the database system from the traditional file based system are the following:

- In the file based system, every subsystem of the information system would have its own set of files to handle its data processing applications i.e., each user creates the files separately based on the specific requirements of data processing. This results a number of disadvantages which include inconsistent data, duplication of data, isolation of data, data dependence and data integrity. However in the database system, data is defined once and maintained in a single repository. The data maintained in a single database minimize the redundancy and inconsistency of data.

- The file based system has a characteristic called as program data dependence. The physical structure and the storage of data files are well defined in the application codes. But in the database system, data is independent of programs.

- In file based systems, each application is free to name data elements independently, where as in a database system, names of data are defined once and used repeatedly by applications.

Benefits of Database Systems

The data in the database system possess various features that are enforced by the DBMS are correctness, consistency, security, sharing, reliable and persistence. The benefits of the database system over the traditional file based system are described below.

- **Controlling data redundancy** – In the file based system, every user group maintains its own files for handling its data processing applications. This may lead to the repetition of storing the same data several times. The data redundancy causes several problems such as possibility of error occurrence due to updating of the data in different files, wastage of storage space when the same data is stored repeatedly, data inconsistency due the presence of the same data in different files. However, in the database system, the data is stored at a single place without redundancy. This results in saving storage space, time and money.

- **Consistency of data** – The data redundancy in the file system approach causes the inconsistency of data, but the controlled redundancy in a database system provides the consistency of data among multiple files.

- **Availability of information** – In a file system, files are maintained separately by each user group. Thus it is difficult to obtain and share the information among the different users. In the database system approach, the information is available to all users. A DBMS makes the database to share and update the information by many users or applications.

- **Authorized access to data** – Applications are developed separately and temporarily based on the requirement of the user in file systems. Thus enforcing security to access data is difficult in such environments. A main objective in developing a database system is to enable many users to access and share the data in a secured manner. The security and authorization system for sharing information among multiple users can be enforced by the DBMS.

- **Data integrity** – Data integrity refers to correctness and accuracy nature of the stored data. The accuracy of data can be achieved by defining the constraints and checks on the entered data. In a file system, imposing of data integrity is not easier due to the separate control of data by each user group. The centralized control of data permits to define integrity constraints on the data by the DBMS in a database system.

- **Data independence** – In a file based system, the application program is dependent on data. Since the description of data and the logic for accessing the data are maintained and built into each application. Database systems separate the data description from data.

- **Reduced application development time** – Developing and maintaining application programs separately takes more time which also forces high cost in a file based system.

Design and development of a multiuser database system for applications using a DBMS takes less time with low cost.

- **Enforcing standards** – Standards define the rules for controlling the access of data in user groups. Enforcing standards in a traditional file system is difficult. The database system approach can enforce standards among database users.

Even though the database system approach provides a number of benefits for managing data, it also gives the limitations which include the following:

- Hardware and software start-up costs.
- Damage to a database system affects the entire application programs.

Characteristics of Database Systems

The main characteristics of a typical database system are the following:

- **Self describing nature** – The database system contains the complete description of the database structure and constraints. The definition is stored in the DBMS catalog which contains information includes the structure of each file, the type and storage format of each data item and various constraints on the data. The information stored in the catalog is called meta-data which describes the structure of the primary database.
- **Program-data independence** – Any changes in the structure of data files do not require changing in the DBMS access programs. Since the structure of data files is stored in the DBMS catalog separately from the access programs.
- **Data abstraction** – A database system provides the conceptual representation of data to the users and hides the storage and implementation details of data. Data model is a type of data abstraction that is used to provide the conceptual representation of data to the users.
- **Multiple views of data** – A database system supports multiple views of data based on the requirement of the different users. Since each user may see a different view of the database, which describes only the data of interest to that user.
- **Data sharing and concurrent access of data** – Database systems allow sharing of data among multiple users and also support simultaneous accessing of database for multiuser transaction processing applications.

1.4.   Characteristics of the DBMS

A typical DBMS provides multiple facilities to access a database in a database system. A DBMS controls access to the data and provides features for database creation, data manipulation, data integrity and data security. The main objectives of a DBMS include an efficient, flexible, reliable and secure management of data. In order to meet these objectives a DBMS can include the software that provides:

- **Data modeling capabilities** – A data model includes a set of predefined constructs for structuring data that can involve predefined data types, basic operations, and user defined data structures. An important aspect of data modeling is the ability of the user to define complex data objects and relationships. A data model also supports the design and use of standardized data representations that can facilitate reuse, exchange of data among applications or users.

- **High-level database language** – A high-level database language (DBL) usually referred to as the query language that provides the interface to the database. The DBL is used directly and interactively for defining, manipulating and querying of data. DBL statements can also be embedded in a host language (the implementation language of the application) for indirectly accessing data in the database. In a DBL, data management is usually specified more declaratively than in a conventional programming language.

- **Persistent storage of data** – Data and program procedures are stored permanently on secondary storage for later retrieval after the termination of program execution. Persistency implies a process of how to store objects as well as a persistence mechanism.

- **Efficient accessibility of data** – The DBMS supports facilities for creating access structures, or indexes, which make access of data elements efficient. There are general indexing techniques such as various tree data structures and hash tables, and techniques specialized for certain types of data, such as quad trees for spatial data. The DBMS usually has facilities for optimizing queries, i.e. transforming a query into a form that has an effective execution order.

- **Improved data integrity** – Database integrity refers to the validity and consistency of stored data. The DBMS can specify integrity in terms of constraints, which are consistency rules that the database is not permitted to violate.

- **Handling of hardware and software failures** – To assure that the database is recovered from various types of hardware and software failures, the DBMS should include the facilities for logging of transactions, making backup of the database, and recovery procedures to recover from failures and restore the database into its last consistent state.

- **Data sharing through concurrency control and transaction processing** – Operations in a DBMS are performed as transactions that are logical operation units on the database. The transaction processing software controls the state of transactions and guarantees that the database has always return to a consistent state. Further, the DBMS can use concurrency control to ensure that several users can access and update the same data element in a controlled manner and guaranteeing a correct result. Thus, transactions and concurrency control ensure multiuser transactions to be performed correctly and several users can share data without bothering about interfering with other users.

- **Access control through authorization** – The DBMS must include authorization mechanisms to access the database in terms of privileges that provide security for protecting the database from unauthorized users.

- **Supports for active behavior** – Enriching database systems with active behavior provide the ability to detect the occurrence of events and respond to them automatically in a timely manner without user intervention. Active behavior of a database is defined through active rules which has in the form of event-condition-action (ECA) rules. A database system coupled with active rules is known as active database system.

- **Support for architecture and applications** –The DBMS should provide an effective architecture for the interaction among the database software components as well as provide the facility for modeling, storing and manipulating complex data that are required by the advanced applications.

Functions of DBMS

The DBMS performs several important functions that guarantee the integrity and consistency of the data in the database. The various functions performed by the DBMS are the following.

- Creates the complex structures required for data storage.
- Allow multiple users to access the data in the network environment.
- Enforces integrity rules to maintain data consistency.
- Stores the definitions of data and their relationships in a data dictionary.
- Provides backup and recovery procedures to ensure data safety.
- Provides security system for authorized accessing of data.
- Provides utility programs and programming language interfaces to access the data.

1.5. Classification of DBMS

DBMSs are complex, sophisticated software applications that provide reliable management of large data. In general DBMSs are classified based on the various criteria such as data model, number of users use the system, database site locations and the type and extent of use.

- **Data model** – A data model which describes the structure of a database. Data model is an abstraction of data and its purpose is to convey the details of the system to software developers. The DBMS is categorized based on the data model are hierarchical, network, relational, object-oriented and object-relational. The main data model used in the commercial DBMS is the object-relational data model.

- **Number of users** – The second criteria used to classify a DBMS is the number of users supported by the system. They are single-user and multiuser systems. Single-user DBMS supports only one user and it is restricted to personal computer systems with no sharing of data. Multiuser DBMS allows many users to access shared data at the same time. The majority of the database management systems support multiuser systems.

- **Database site locations** – The third criteria is the number of site locations over which the database is distributed. The different database systems on the basis of database site locations are centralized DBMS, distributed DBMS. The centralized DBMS can support multiple users, but the DBMS software and the database reside totally at a single computer location. A distributed DBMS can have the actual database and DBMS software distributed over many locations, connected by a computer network.

- **Type and extent of use** – A DBMS is classified based on the types of access path for storing files. A DBMS can be designed as either general purpose or special purpose based on its use. A special purpose DBMS is designed for a specific application and it cannot be used for other applications. For example, railway reservation system is a specific application which uses special purpose DBMS for processing concurrent transactions to reserve tickets.

1.6. Categories of Users in Database Systems

Many people are involved in the design, development, maintenance and use of a database system.

In general, the two groups of people involved in the database system environment are database system users and database system developers.

1.6.1. Database System Users

Based on the nature of the role played by the people, the different types of database system users are:

- **Database administrator (DBA)** – The DBA is the administrator, who is responsible for managing the database resources such as the database and the DBMS software. The DBA is also responsible for authorizing database access to the users, coordinating and monitoring the database use and acquiring software and hardware resources as required. The DBA is accountable for problems such as security threats and poor system response time. In order to carry out these functions, the DBA is assisted by a staff in large organizations.

- **Database designer** – A Database designer is responsible for identifying the data to be stored in the database and for choosing appropriate structure to represent and store the data. A Database designer is also responsible to interact with all perspective of database users and understand their requirements for creating a database design that satisfy the requirements of all user groups.

- **End users** – End users are the people whose role is to access the database for getting data. The various categories of end users are:

  a) **Casual users** – These users need different information each time and occasionally access the database. They use sophisticated query language to specify their requests. Casual users need to learn only a few facilities of the DBMS that they use repeatedly.

  b) **Naive Users** – These users constantly query and update the database using standard types of queries to perform their tasks. Naive users need to learn the user interface facilities provided by the DBMS. For example bank tellers and reservation agents are called as the naive users of the database. Bank tellers check account balances and post deposits and withdrawals. Reservation agents check the availability of seats to make reservation.

  c) **Standalone users** – These users maintain personal databases and use GUI based prewritten packages to perform their tasks. Standalone users need to learn most of the facilities of the DBMS for their use. For example, tax calculation package provides the facility to calculate tax of an employee in an organization.

  d) **Sophisticated users** – These users are well familiar with the facilities of the DBMS and develop their own applications based on their requirements.

Business analysts, engineers, and scientists are the examples of sophisticated users.

- **System analyst**s – System analysts determine the requirements of end users and develop specifications for standard transactions. These people should familiar with all capabilities provided by the DBMS.

- **Application programmers** – These people implement the specifications specified by the analysts as programs. Application programmers are also called as software engineers should well familiar with all DBMS facilities.

1.6.2. Database System Developers

In addition to the people those who administer, design and use a database, another category of people associated with the design, development and maintenance of the DBMS software and system environment are the following:

- **DBMS designers and implementers** – Design and implement the DBMS software package for database system users.

- **Tool developers** – Design and implement tools that facilitate database modeling, database design, performance monitoring, graphical interfaces, prototyping and test data generation.

- **Maintenance personnel** – These people are responsible for the maintenance of hardware and software environment of the database system.

1.7. Applications of Database Systems

Database systems are important for many applications ranging from commercial problems to space station operations. Generally, database systems are accessed either by the user program or an application. Users interact with the database system by executing applications, where each application consists of set of operations to be performed on the stored data. Database application stores its data in a database and uses the services of a DBMS to retrieve and update the data and also to protect and maintain its integrity. Database applications construct and submit transactions to manipulate the persistent data stored by a DBMS.

Database systems are useful in real-time applications because they combine several features that facilitate (i) the description of data, (ii) the maintenance of correctness and integrity of the data, (iii) efficient access to the data and (iv) the correct executions of query and transaction execution in spite of concurrency and failures.

Traditionally database systems are used to manage structured data that arises in routine applications in banking, insurance, finance and manufacturing. Database systems now provide comprehensive facilities for modeling both structural and behavioral aspects of applications like object-oriented applications which includes engineering design, multimedia publishing and manufacturing systems. Database systems are used for many application domains such as engineering, medicine and information retrieval system. Some of the example applications are the following:

- Scientific applications that store large amounts of data resulting from scientific experiments in areas such as engineering and medical domains.
- Image processing applications that store and retrieve images in areas such as satellite photographic images and images from medical procedures such as x-rays and magnetic resonance imaging (MRI).
- Spatial applications that store spatial location of data such as weather information, automobile navigation systems and maps used in geographical information systems (GIS).
- Time series applications that store information such as economic data at regular points in time and stock of products.
- Data mining applications that analyze large amount of data searching for identifying patterns and relationships in areas such as customer personal interests and social networking groups.
- Business process applications that store persistent data stores for enforcing transactional semantics.

1.8. Summary

This chapter has discussed the basic concepts of database systems. This chapter has provided the definition of database system, components of database manager and the benefits of database approach over the traditional file based system. This chapter has explained the various characteristics and classification of the DBMS. In addition, this chapter has described the various categories of people involved in the design, development, maintenance and use of a database system. In the end this chapter has presented the use of database systems in various application domains.

Review Questions

1. Define database, DBMS and database systems.
2. What are the four elements of a database system?
3. Explain the features and facilities provided by the DBMS.
4. Write the various components of a database system environment.

5. Describe the benefits of database systems over the traditional file based system.

6. What are the main characteristics of a database system?

7. Discuss the characteristics of the DBMS.

8. Write the functions of DBMS.

9. Explain the various criteria used for classifying the DBMS.

10. What are the responsibilities of database administrator?

11. Write about the different types of database system end-users.

12. What are the database system features useful in database applications?

13. Write down the various applications of database systems.

References

1. L.B. Bergholt, J.S. Due, R.T. Hohn, J.L. Knudsen, K.H. Nielsen, T.S. Olesen and E.H. Pedersen, "Database Management Systems: Relational, Object-Relational, and Object-Oriented Data models", Center for Object Technology, COT/4-02-V1.1, Pp.1-120, 1998.

2. T.M. Connolly and C.E. Begg, "Database Systems: A Practical Approach to Design, Implementation, and Management", Fourth Edition, Pearson Education Ltd, 2012.

3. R. Elmasri, S. Navathe, "Database Systems: Models, Languages, Design and Application Programming", Sixth edition, Pearson Education Ltd, 2013.

CHAPTER 2

DATABASE MODELS AND ARCHITECTURE

Key Features

- Data Models
- Entity-Relationship (ER) Model
- Relational Data Model
- Object-Oriented Data Model
- Object-Relational Data Model
- Database System Architecture
- Database Schema, State and Data Independence

2.1. Introduction

In order to accommodate the requirements of advanced database applications, database systems should provide the various features such as data modeling capabilities, persistent storage of data, efficient accessibility of data, improved data integrity, handling of hardware and software failures, access control through authorization, support for architecture and applications.

The main characteristic of the database approach is to support data abstraction that helps different users to perceive the data at their preferred level. A data model which describes the structure of the database helps in achieving data abstraction. This chapter explains the various data models which include conceptual, representational and physical data models. Entity-Relationship (ER) model is the most popular high-level conceptual data model which is used to facilitate conceptual database design. ER diagrams are used to represent the ER model. Representational database models are the methodology used by a particular DBMS to organize and access data. The various types of representational data models suggested are fall under the category of either record based or object based models. This chapter explains the three important representational data models such as relational, object-oriented and object-relational data models. Physical data models describe how data is stored as files in the computer by representing information such as record formats, record orderings and access paths.

Also this chapter provides the concept of database system architecture. The database system architecture is a framework, in which the structure of the DBMS is described. This chapter describes the two different architectural approaches for DBMS such as structure of a DBMS that provides various components to perform functions to its users and ANSI three-level architecture which includes the external, conceptual and internal levels to provide three different views of the data in database. Also this chapter presents client/server architecture which is the most common and flexible architecture that is used to implement multiuser database management system.

This chapter describes the concept of database schema, database state and data independence. The overall description of a database is called the database schema. The data in the database at a particular moment in time is called a database state. Data independence provides the capacity to change the schema at one level of a database system without having to change the schema at the next higher level.

2.2. Data Models

Database models present a process of abstracting the static and dynamic attributes of real world entities. A data model is an abstraction of data that helps in the understanding of the structure of database. The structure of the database implies data types, relationships and constraints that apply to the data. The purpose of building a data model is to organize the data in a database.

Types of Data Models

The various types of data models are developed based on the concepts they use to describe the database structure. They are:

- **Conceptual data models** give the comprehensive view of the entire database. Entity-Relationship (ER) model is the most popular high-level conceptual data model which provides concepts such as entities, attributes and their relationships to model the database based on the user requirements. The ER model is commonly used for the conceptual design of database applications.

- **Representational data models** define the data structure along with the relationships between the data elements. A representational database model specifies particular mechanism for data storage and retrieval. The various well known representational data models implemented in database systems are relational, object-oriented and object-relational data models.

- **Physical data models** describe how data is stored as files in the computer by representing information such as record formats, record orderings and access paths. An access path is a structure that makes the search for particular database records efficient. An index is an example of an access path that allows direct access to data using an index term or keyword.

2.3.   Entity-Relationship Model

Entity-Relationship (ER) model is a high level conceptual data model which is used to facilitate database design. A conceptual model is independent of the particular databases and hardware environment that is used to implement the database. ER data model is the most widely used model to carry out the conceptual design of the database.

The ER model is represented by **ER diagrams** that allow the user to describe the data in a real world enterprise in terms of objects called as entities and their relationships. ER diagrams provide a visual, graphical model of information content of a system. Database designers create ER diagrams that represent their understanding of the user requirements.

2.3.1.   Components of ER Model

The ER model provides various components that allow the user to specify the conceptual design of the database. The various components of the ER model are the following.

- **Entity** – An entity is a thing or object in the real world that is distinguishable from other objects. An entity is identified by a name and described using properties or attributes.
- **Attribute** – An attribute is a characteristic of an entity or relationship. The various types of attributes are simple, composite, single-valued, multi-valued and derived.
  - A simple attribute is an attribute composed of a single component with an independent existence. Simple attributes cannot be further subdivided. For example, employee number, name and department.
  - An attribute composed of multiple components, each of which independent existence is called composite attribute. For example, address attribute is composed of components like street name, city and pin code.
  - A single-valued attribute is one that holds a single value for an entity. In general for a particular entity, majority of attributes are single-valued.
  - A multi-valued attribute is one that holds multiple values for an entity. For example, student entity has multiple values for the attribute 'hobbies' such as reading, playing instrument.
  - A derived attribute is one that represents a value that is derivable from the value of a related attribute. For example, the age attribute is derived from the related attribute date-of-birth.

- **Domain** – Each attribute is associated with a set of values called a domain. The domain defines the potential values that an attribute may hold.

- **Entity set** – An entity set is a collection of entities of the same type that share same attributes. Each entity set has a distinguished set of attributes called a key that can be used to uniquely identify each entity. There can be more than one candidate key and use one of them as primary key. The two types of entity sets are strong entity sets and weak entity sets. An entity set that has a primary key is considered as a strong entity and is not dependent on some other entity. A weak entity has not sufficient attributes to form a primary key and is dependent on some other entity.

  For example, Figure 2.1 shows the ER diagram representation of Employee entity with simple attributes such as Emp-code, Emp-name and Designation and Emp-code is the primary key. In ER diagrams, entity is represented by a rectangle and attributes are represented by an oval. The primary key attribute is underlined.

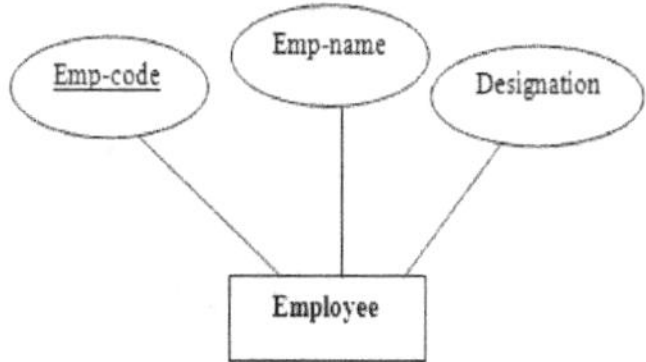

Figure 2.1: Employee Entity

- **Relationships** – Entities have relationships to one another. A relationship is an association between two or more entities. The relationship that exists among the entities relates data items to each other in a meaningful way. For example, the relationship exists between an employee (entity) works-in (relationship) the sales department (entity).

- **Relationship set** – A Relationship set is a collection of relationships that relate entities from the same entity sets. A relationship set can also have descriptive attributes.

  For example, Figure 2.2 shows the ER diagram for a relationship Works-in which exists between the two entities, Employee and Department with Since as the descriptive attribute. In ER diagram, a relationship is represented by a diamond symbol.

- **Degree** – The degree of a relationship indicates the number of entities associated in the relationship. The various degrees of relationship are unary, binary, ternary and quaternary relationships. A unary relationship exists when an association is maintained within a single entity as shown in Figure 2.1. A binary relationship exists when two entities are associated. For example in Figure 2.2, the degree of relationship between entities is binary since two entities are associated with a relationship Works-in.

A ternary relationship exists when there are three entities associated. For example, in a company database domain the ternary relationship occurs when the three entities such as Employee, Department and Location are associated using Works-in relationship. The ternary relationship can get by associating Locations entity with Works-in relationships in Figure 2.2.

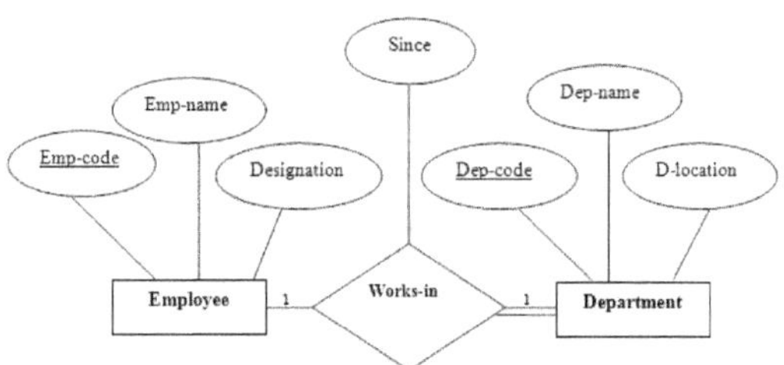

Figure 2.2: Works-in Relationships

The entity set that participate in a relationship set need not be distinct and a relationship can involve two entities in the same entity set. For example, consider the Reports-to relationship that is shown in Figure 2.3. Here employees report to other employees, every relationship in Repots-to is of the form (emp1, emp2), where both emp1 and emp2 are entities in Employees. But both entities play different roles, emp1 reports to the managing employee emp2 which is specified in the role indicators such as Subordinate and Supervisor respectively in Figure 2.3.

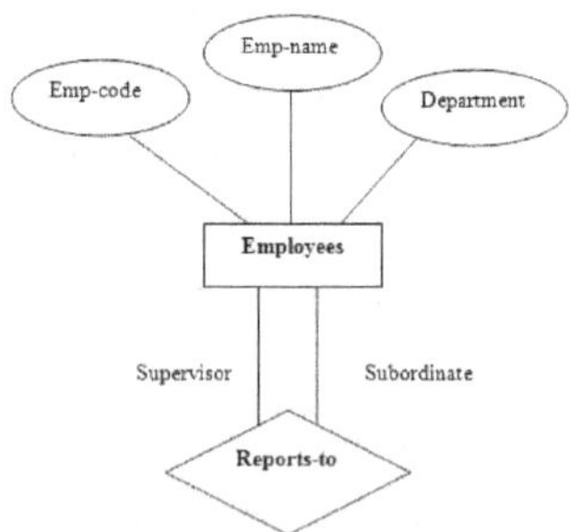

Figure 2.3: Reports-to Relationship

- **Relationship constraints** – Relationship constraints limit the possible number of entities that may participate in the corresponding relationship set. The two types of relationship constraints are cardinality ratio and participation.

  1. **Cardinality Ratio:** Cardinality ratio represents the way the entities are related. It is a representation of the business policies established by the user or enterprise. The cardinality of a relationship appears as the maximum values for the multiplicity ranges on either side of a relationship. The most common degree for relationships is binary. The cardinality ratios for a binary relationship are the following:

     - **One-to-One (1:1)** – An entity in A is associated with utmost one entity in B and an entity in B is associated with at most one entity in A. For example, a 1:1 binary relationship 'Manages' is shown in Figure 2.4 which relates a department entity to the employee entity who manages the department. This represents the constraint that, at any point in time, an employee can manage one department only and a department can have one manger only.

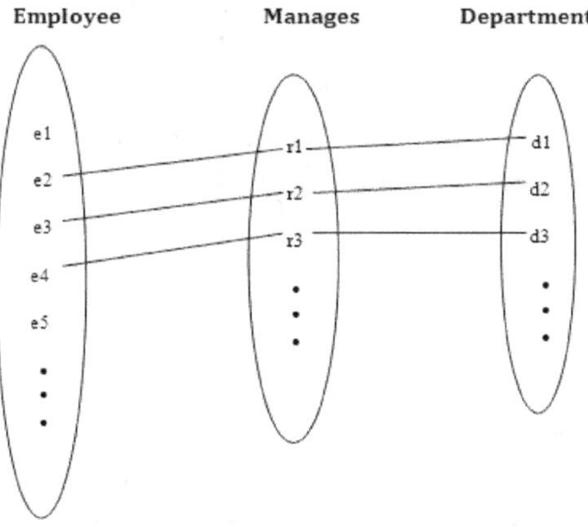

Figure 2.4: 1:1 relationship, Manages

     - **One-to-Many (1: N)** – An entity in A is associated with any number of entities in B. However an entity in B can be associated with at most one entity in A. For example, in Figure 2.5, the Works-for binary relationship between Department: Employee is of cardinality ratio 1:N, meaning that each department can be related to any number of employees, but an employee can be related to (work-for) only one department.

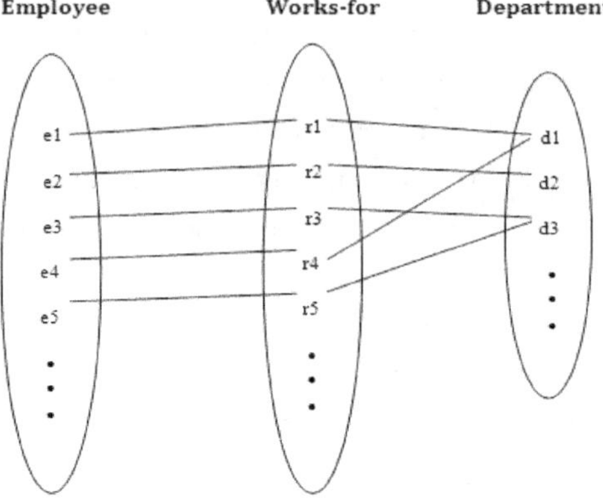

Figure 2.5: 1: N relationship, Works-for

- **Many-to-Many (M:N)** – An entity in A is associated with any number of entities in B and an entity in B is also associated with any number of entities in A. For example, the relationship type Works-on, as shown in Figure 2.6 is of cardinality ratio M:N, since the constraint is that an employee can work on several projects and a project can have several employees.

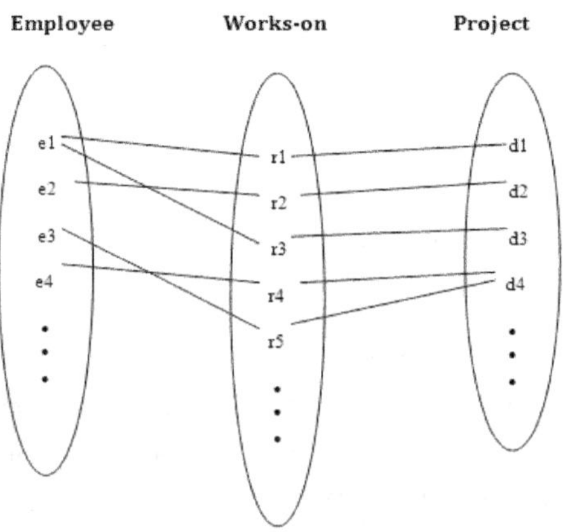

Figure 2.6: M:N Relationship, Works-on

2. **Participation Constraints:** The participation constraint represents whether all entity occurrences are involved in a particular relationship or only some. The two types of participation constraint are total or partial. The participation of entities in a relationship appears as minimum values for the multiplicity ranges on either side of the relationship. Optional participation is represented as minimum value of 0 while mandatory participation is shown as maximum value of 1. In Figure 2.5, the participation of Employee entity in Works-for relationship is an example of total participation constraint. Since the business policy states that every employee must work for department, then an employee entity can exist only if it participates in at least one Works-for relationship. However the participation of Employee entity in the Manages relationship as shown in Figure 2.4 is an example of partial constraint. Here the part of the employee entity is related to some department entity through Manages, but not all.

2.3.2. *Notations Used in ER Diagrams*

ER diagrams enable the database designers and users to express their understanding of what the planned database is intended to do and communicate their requirements through a common language.

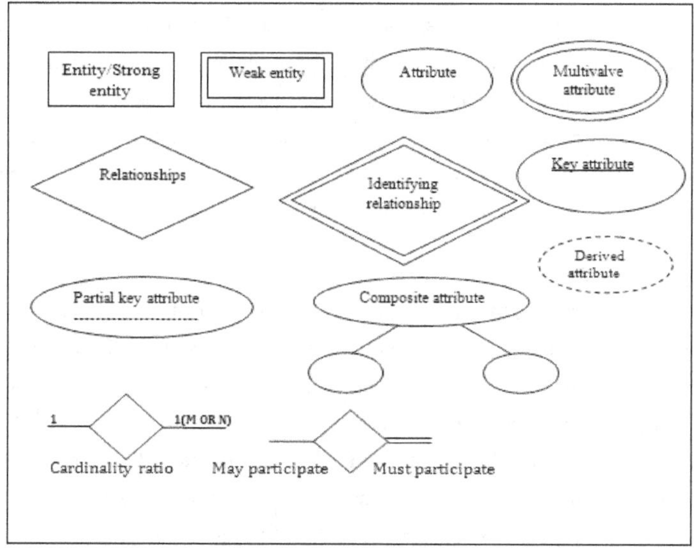

Figure 2.7: ER Diagram Notations

In general, various ER diagram notations such as Chen notation and Crow's Feet notation are used to represent ER models. A diagrammatic notation that uses an increasingly popular object-oriented language called the unified modeling language (UML) is also used to create ER models.

The ER diagram notations based on Chen model is shown in Figure 2.7. The entities are represented by a rectangular box with the name of the entity. The various types of attributes are simple, single-valued, multi-valued, composite and derived attributes. A single-valued or simple attribute is represented as an oval with attribute name and is attached to a relevant entity by a line. The primary key attribute is underlined. The multi-valued attribute is represented as a double lined oval and the derived attribute is represented as a dotted line oval. If the attribute is composite, its component attributes are shown as emanating from the composite attribute. The relationship is represented using a diamond notation with relationship name. The weak entity set is represented as a double lined rectangle. The cardinality and participation constraints are specified beside the entity. The ER diagram examples shown in section 2.3.1 use the Chen notation to represent the ER model.

2.4.   Representational Data Models

An important aspect in DBMS evolution is the development sophisticated database models. Data are structured and organized in databases with respect to data model. Database models provide a way in which the stored data is organized as specified structure for quick access and efficient management. The major difference between the different database models lies in the modes of specifying relationships and constraints among the data elements.

Representational database models are the methodology used by a particular DBMS to organize and access data. The various types of representational data models suggested are fall under the category of either record based or object based models.

Record Based Models

In a record based model, the database consists of a number of fixed format records with different types. Each record type defines a fixed number of fields with a fixed length for each. Record based data models are used to specify the overall structure of the database and a higher level description of the implementation.

The three types of record based data models are hierarchical data model, network data model and relational data model. In hierarchical data model, data are represented by records and relationships among data are represented by links. The records are organized as collection of trees and a record type can be owned by only the owner. The structure of hierarchical data model resembles the structure chart, showing levels of hierarchy representing parent-child relationship and each level represents record. For example, in shopping system, orders are owned by only one customer.

In network model, data are represented by collections of records and relationships among data are represented by links. The records in the database are organized as generalized graph structures. In this model records appearing as nodes and relationships are the edges in the graph. The network model consists of collection of set-type occurrences. In supply-chain application system, Salesman–Customer and Supplier–Parts are examples of network data model. In the relational model, data are represented as collection of relations. A relation is a two dimensional table structure with columns and rows and it stores collection of related entities. Relations are related or linked to each other by data fields. For example, in shopping system, customer relation and order relation are linked by comparing data fields.

Object Based Models

Object based models use the concept of object technology for specifying the structure of the database. The object based model consists of static properties such as objects, attributes and relationships and dynamic properties such as operations defining new database states based on applied state changes. Thus the object based data models are used to express the static and dynamic properties of data as well as the operations over objects. The two important object based data models used in the database systems are the object-oriented and object-relational data models. Object-oriented data model extends the attribute property that describes both the state and the behavior of the object and it also captures the semantics of objects with object oriented programming concepts. Object-relational model extends the relational model with the support of object-oriented programming features such as encapsulation, inheritance, class definitions and support for complex unstructured data.

The important representational data models that are used in the research and commercial database systems are: relational model, object-oriented data model and object-relational data model. These data models are described in the following sections.

2.4.1. Relational Data Model

The relational data model was introduced in 1970 by E.M.Codd and it is the most wide spread data model for database applications. The relational data model is based on a mathematical foundation, called relational algebra. Relational data model deals with the data aspect of information models and ignoring the dynamic or behavioral aspects of information modeling. In the relational data model, information is organized in relations using the form of two-dimensional tables. Each relation contains a set of tuples (records). Each tuple contain a number of fields. A field may contain a simple value (fixed or variable size) based on the domain. Relational modeling focuses on the information in the system and not on the behavior. The modeling dimension has accomplished in relational database systems through well defined aspects like domain, relation, tuple, attribute, relation values, relation keys, views and normal forms.

The major advantages of relational model are structural dependence, conceptual simplicity, easy of design, implementation and maintenance, ad-hoc query capability. The disadvantage of this model is the lack of handling of objects. The only data structure supported by the relational data model is the relation. Thus information about a complex object is scattered over many relations, which leads to a loss of direct correspondence between real world object and its database representation. Several commercial database systems implement relational model. The various commercial relational DBMSs such as DB2 and Informix Dynamic Server from IBM, Sybase DBMS from Sybase, Oracle from Oracle Corporation, SQL server and Access from Microsoft and several open source systems such as MySQL and Postgre SQL are developed based on the relational model.

2.4.2. *Object-Oriented Data Model*

Object-oriented data model deals with both the data and the dynamic and behavioral aspects of data modeling. In the object-oriented data model, information is organized in terms of objects, where each object has a number of attributes. Attributes are simple values, complex values, references to other objects, or methods. Objects are instances of classes, and classes are related to each by means of inheritance. The inheritance mechanism supports generalization and specialization and offers many aspects of structured reuse of models. Inheritance also offers the mechanism for qualified polymorphism, since the resulting type system can allow objects to be recognized as belonging to several different types. A method of an object is a specification of functionality, typically manipulations of the attributes in the same object.

The various advantages of using object-oriented data model are: support for handling complex data types with object-oriented programming features, reusability of objects and methods, notion of enforcing semantic integrity constraints for attaching different meanings to generic data types.

The main disadvantage of this model is the lack of standard and thus it is not compatible with other models. The various commercial object-oriented DBMSs such as Jasmine from Computer Associates, Gemstone's Gemstone, O2's O2 and Object Design's Object Store are developed based on the object-oriented model.

2.4.3. *Object-Relational Data Model*

Object-relational data model combines the benefits of both relational and object-oriented data model. This model extends the relational model with the support of object-oriented programming features such as encapsulation, inheritance, class definitions and support for complex unstructured data.

An object-relational model can be thought of as a relational model where tables are considered as classes, tuples are object instantiations of classes, and columns of tables are attributes of their corresponding classes. Class inheritance is supported by allowing tables (sub tables) to inherit all or certain columns, constraints and storage options of other tables. Within an object-relation model, attribute domains are abstract data types (ADTs), user-defined data types (UDTs) or any of the data types supported in relational model. ADTs are data types constructed from other built in data types (integer, string, char etc.). UDTs are data types whose internal structures are completely opaque to the database and the database has no intrinsic mechanism to access such data. Therefore all UDTs must be accompanied by user-defined access methods for reading, writing, indexing and querying information within them. Encapsulation is supported by this model when methods are assigned to tables and serve as mechanisms through which users can access and manipulate table attributes. As like relational model, tables can have constraints, storage options, indexes, methods and triggers.

The various advantages of using object-relational data model are: exploitation of large relational user-based technologies and standards, enforcement of semantic integrity constraints, no interface mismatch problem for storing object-oriented data and support for complex data types. The disadvantages of this model are: difference in implementation among vendors to support for user defined data types and data type extensions. However these difficulties are rectified by the SQL3 standard. The SQL3 standard provide a complete model for managing persistent objects and also provide vendors with a neutral model for implementing portable database environments. Oracles 8.x from Oracle, Universal Server (Illustra) from Informix, Universal Database from IBM are the various commercial object-relational DBMSs that use object-relational data model.

2.4.4. *Comparison of Database Models*

The Table 2.1 summarizes the characteristics comparison of five database models based on the features such as data representation, data relationship and data model category. Data representation specifies how the data elements are physically organized in the database. Data relationship refers the representation of relationship between the data elements. The category of data models are either record based or object based models. The record based model supports fixed format records with different types where as the object based model uses the concept of object technology for specifying the structure of the database.

Table 2.1: Comparison of Database Models

Features	Data Models				
	Hierarchical	Network	Relational	Object-Oriented	Object-Relational
Data representation	Records	Collections of Records	Relations in the form of two-dimensional table	Objects with attributes	Extends tables with object-oriented features
Data relationship	Links	Links	Data fields specified as number of columns with unique name	Properties and operations of data over objects	Table fields are considered as classes. Records are object instantiations of classes and columns are attributes of their classes
Data model category	Record Based	Record based	Record based	Object based	Object based

2.5.   Database System Architecture

The database system architecture is a framework in which the structure of the DBMS is described. The way the components of the DBMS work together to achieve certain goals is referred as the structure or system architecture.

The different framework approaches for DBMS are suggested based on: (i) the functions that the components of a DBMS must provide to its users (ii) different views of data (or levels of abstraction) that are possible within the database. A commonly used view of data is the three-level architecture.

Based on the first approach, the simplified view of a database system structure is shown in Figure 2.8 which consists of the various components such as users/application programmers, application interfaces/ programs, DBMS and database. The DBMS accepts input commands generated from a variety of user interfaces, produces evaluation plans, executes these plans against the database and returns the answers.

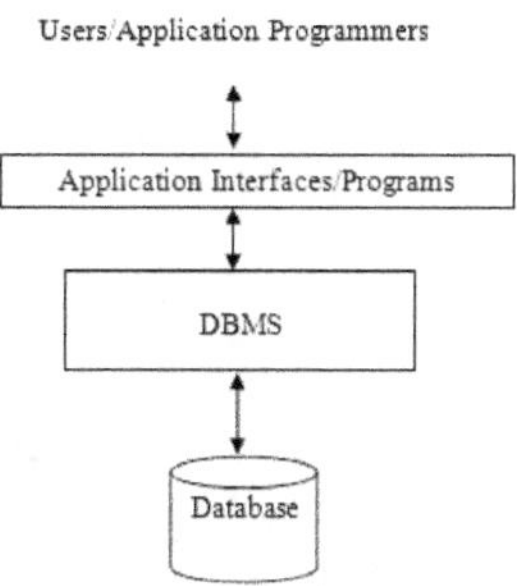

Figure 2.8: Simplified Structure of Database System

2.5.1. *Three-Level Architecture of DBMS*

The data in a DBMS is described at three levels of abstraction based on the ANSI/SPARC architecture. The three levels of data abstraction are the three different views of the data in a database which is known as three-level architecture that includes the external, conceptual and internal levels. The way the users' perceive the data is called the external level. The conceptual level provides mapping and the desired independence between the external and internal levels. The way the DBMS and the operating system perceive the data is the internal level, where the data is actually stored using the data structures and the file organizations.

The goal of the three-level architecture is to separate each user's view of the database system from the way the database is physically represented. The three levels form a three-level architecture comprising an external, conceptual and an internal level is shown in Figure 2.9.

External or View Level

The external level has number of external schemas which describes that part of the database that is relevant to each user. The external level is the users' view of the database. This level provides a view which allows the user (application program or end user) to see only the data of interest to them. This level deals with the way data is stored and presented to users. This level describes how the data in the database is perceived by users and it is not concerned with how data is handled and processed by the DBMS. Since a database is a shared resource, each user may require different views of the data held in the database. Users are shielded from the way data is stored on the underlying system and manipulate the data without worrying about where it is located and how it is actually stored. In general, the end users and application programmers are interested in an external view of the database.

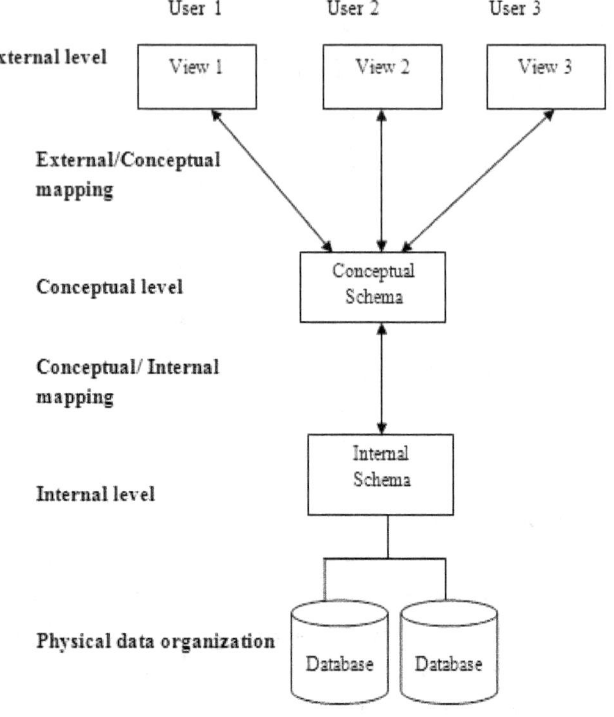

Figure 2.9: Three-Level Architecture

Conceptual Level

The conceptual level has a conceptual schema which presents a community view of the entire database. This level describes the stored data and the relationships among the data in the database. The conceptual level is a complete view of the data requirements of the organization and is independent of DBMS. This level represents all entities with their attributes, relationships between entities, constraints on the data, semantic information about the data, security and integrity information.

Internal or Physical Level

The internal level describes the physical storage structure of the database. The collection of files permanently stored on secondary storage device is known as the physical storage. This level provides a low-level description of the physical database and an interface between the operating file system and the record structures used in higher levels of abstraction. The internal level has an internal schema which provides the view about the physical storage of data. The internal view does not directly deal with the physical devices instead it views a physical device as a collection of physical pages and allocates space in terms of logical pages.

The three-level ANSI architecture is important in database system development because it clearly separates the users' external level, the systems conceptual level, and internal storage level for designing a database. The three schemas are only description of the data and the stored data is actually exists at the physical level. In a DBMS based on the three schema architecture, each user group refers only to its own external schema into a request against the conceptual schema, and then into a request on the internal schema for processing over the stored database. If the request is database retrieval, the data extracted from the stored database must be reformatted to match the user's external view. The processes of transforming requests and results between levels are called mappings.

2.5.2. Client/Server DBMS Architecture

The construction of high performance database systems that combine the aspects of relational and object-oriented approaches require the design of flexible architecture that can fully exploit the resources available in the system. The most common and flexible architecture that is used to implement multiuser database management system is client/server (C/S) architecture. The C/S architecture refers to the way in which software components interact. Client and servers are the separate logical entities that are connected over the computer network to perform a specific task. A client is a user machine that provides user interface capabilities and local processing. A server is a system that can provide services to the client machines such as file access, database access and web access. A client is connected to the server through a middleware component. Middleware is software that connects the client to the server for allowing the clients to access data from server.

The C/S architecture of a database system has two logical components namely client and server, each executes on different systems and are connected into a network. The client process that requires certain resource and the server process that provides the resource. The applications and tools act as clients of the DBMS and the DBMS software act as the server. The client takes the user's request, checks the syntax and generates the database requests appropriate to the application logic and then it transmits the message to the server, waits for response and formats the response for the end-user. The server accepts and processes the database requests, then transmits the results back to the client. Thus in the C/S database systems, the user interface programs and application programs can run on client side and the transaction functionality related to SQL processing can run on server side. When DBMS access is required, the middleware program such as Open Database Connectivity (ODBC) provides an application programming interface (API) which allows the client program to call the database server. Also a related standard for the java programming language called JDBC (Java Database Connectivity) is defined to allow Java client programs to access DBMS.

The C/S architecture for DBMS is traditionally designed with two-tier and three-tier model. The two-tier client/server model consists of the client (tier-1) responsible to handle user interface actions and the business application logic and a DBMS or database server (tier-2). Thus in two-tier architecture, there are only two tiers namely client and database server. A generalized view of two-tier C/S database systems is shown in Figure 2.10.

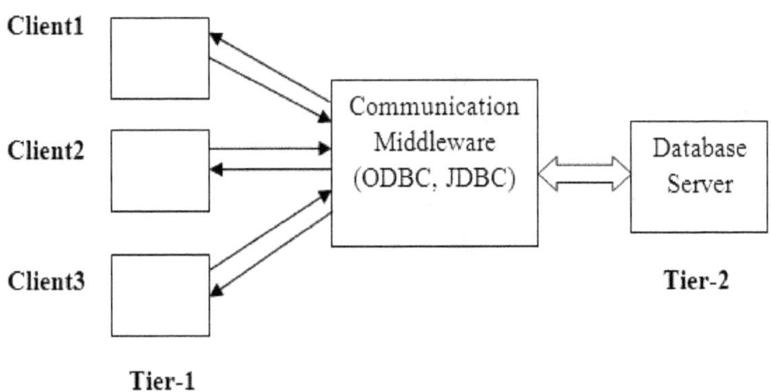

Figure 2.10: Two-tier C/S Database Systems

The need for enterprise scalability and the complexity of advanced applications, two-tier client/server model is improved by the three-tier architecture. The three-tier client/server model consists of a client (tier 1) responsible for user interface, business logic or application server (tier-2) and a DBMS or database server (tier-3).

A generalized view of three-tier C/S database systems is shown in Figure 2.11. In this system there are two servers, namely database server and application server. The application server forms the business logic which can hold the local database and the database server can hold enterprise database. In this architecture, application code is stored in the application server in addition to the local database. The application server which is also called middleware provides the requested resources by calling on another server. The database server provides the data to the application server. Thus in three-tier architecture, the performance of the application system is improved by means of using business or application tier.

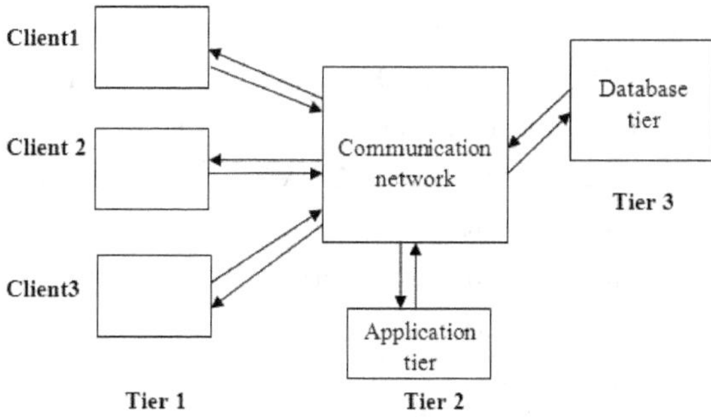

Figure 2.11: Three-Tier C/S Database Systems

2.6.   Database Schema, State and Data Independence

Database Schema

In any data model, it is important to differentiate between the description of the database and the database itself. The description of a database is called as the database schema. The schema is specified during database design process and is not expected to change frequently. However actual data in the database may change frequently. Certain conventions are used for displaying schemes as diagrams by most data models. A displayed schema is called a schema diagram. The schema diagram displays certain aspects of a schema such as the names of record types and data items.   For example, Figure 2.12 shows the schema diagram for student database. The example schema diagram shows the structure of each record type but not the actual instances of records. Each object in the STUDENT schema is called a schema construct.

STUDENT

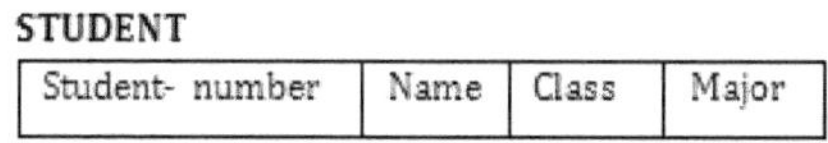

Student- number	Name	Class	Major

Figure 2.12: Schema Diagram for Student Database

The DBMS stores the descriptions of the schema constructs called as meta-data in the DBMS catalog for reference whenever it needs to. Schema can be changed occasionally based on the changes in application requirements which are called as schema evolution. In the STUDENT schema as shown in Figure 2.12, the insertion of data item, percentage of marks is a simple example of schema evolution. The schema of a database system is described in a formal language supported by the DBMS. In a relational database the schema defines the tables, the fields in each table, and the relationship between fields and tables. Generally schemas are stored in a data dictionary.

The three different levels of schema in the database that are defined based on the abstraction of the three-level architecture are external schema, conceptual schema and internal schema. The external schema describes different views of the data. The conceptual schema describes all the entities, attributes and relationships together with integrity constraints. The internal schema is a complete description of the internal model, containing stored records, the data fields, indexes and storage structures are used. The DBMS is responsible for mapping between these three types of schema and it must also check the consistency of the schema.

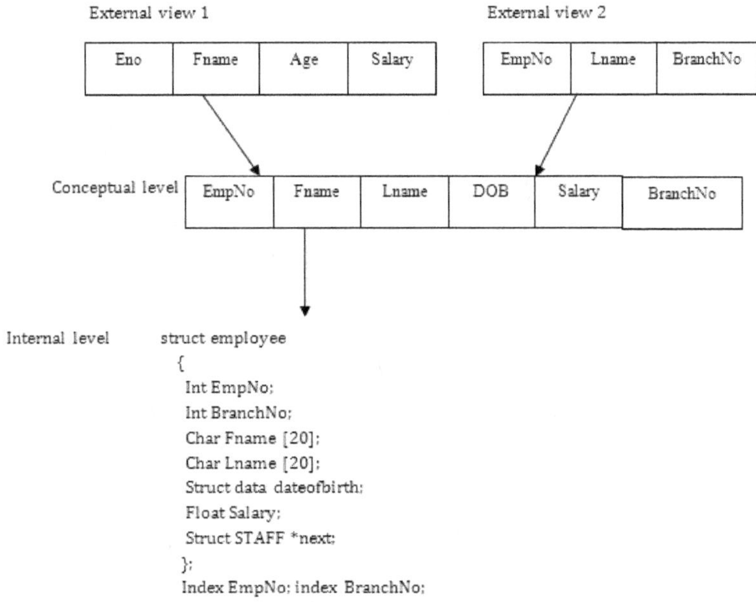

Figure 2.13: Different Levels of Employee Schema

An example of different levels of schema for employee is shown in Figure 2.13. In this example the two external views of employee details exist. These external views are merged into one conceptual schema. In this merging process, the major difference is that, the age field is changed into a date-of-birth (DOB) field. The DBMS maintains the external/conceptual mapping. For example, it maps the Eno field of the first external view to EmpNo field of the conceptual record. The conceptual level is then mapped to the internal level, which contains a physical description of the structure for the conceptual record. At this level, the definition of the structure in a high-level language contains a pointer, next which allows the list of employee records to be physically linked together to form a chain. The order of fields in the internal level is different from that at the conceptual level. Again, the DBMS maintains the conceptual/ internal mapping.

Database State

The actual data in a database is changed every time when the user wants to modify the data. The data in the database at a particular moment in time is called a database state or snapshot. It is also called the current set of occurrences or instances in the database. In a given database state, each schema has its own current set of instances. In a given database state, each schema construct has its own current set of instances. For example, the STUDENT schema shown in Figure 2.12 can contain the set of individual student records as its instances. Many database states can be constructed to correspond to a particular database schema. Every time the user inserts or delete or modify the value of a data in a record, the state of the database is changed to another state.

The difference between database schema and database state is important. Whenever a new database is created, the database schema is specified to the DBMS and the corresponding database state is empty state with no data. The DBMS is partly responsible for ensuring the every state of the database. A database is said to be in a valid state that satisfies the structure specified in the schema. Thus specifying a correct schema to the DBMS is important and the schema should be designed with care. The DBMS stores the descriptions of the schema constructs and constraints also called the meta-data in the DBMS catalog, so that the DBMS can refer to the schema whenever it needs to.

Data Independence

The three-level architecture is used to provide the concept of data independence which is defined as, the capacity to change the schema at one level of a database system without having to change the schema at the next higher level. The two types of data independence are logical and physical. Logical data independence refers the capacity to change the conceptual schema without having to change external schemas. Changes to the conceptual schema may be needed to expand the database and to change constraints. Physical data independence refers the capacity to change the internal schema without having to change the conceptual schema. Hence the external schemas need not be changed. Changes to the internal schema may be needed to reorganize the physical files for creating additional access structures and improving the performance of retrieval or update operations.

2.7. Summary

This chapter has explained the main concepts of database systems which include data models, database system architecture, database schema, database state and data independence. The three main categories of data models such as conceptual, representational and physical data models are discussed. This chapter has presented the two different architectural frameworks for DBMS include the structure and the three levels of abstraction based on ANSI architecture. The ANSI three-level architecture comprised of external, conceptual and internal levels provides the three different views of data in the database. The external level provides the views of different user groups. The conceptual level describes high level description of the whole database and the internal level describes the physical storage structure of the database. The DBMS included the mapping processes to transform requests and results from one level to the next.

This chapter has also described the concept of two-types of client/server architecture for database systems. This chapter has presented the concept of database schema, database state and data independence. The schema does not change very often; where as database state changes every time the data is inserted, modified or deleted. Data independence is defined as the capacity to change the schema at one level of a database system without having to change the schema at the next higher level.

Review Questions

1. What is a data model?
2. What are the various types of data models?
3. Write a note on Entity-Relationship (ER) model.
4. What is ER diagram?
5. Write the concept of record-based and object based data models.
6. Explain the relational data model.
7. Describe about object-oriented data model.
8. What are the advantages of object-oriented data model?
9. What are the disadvantages of object-oriented data model?
10. Explain the object-relational data model.
11. Write the advantages of object-relational data model.
12. What is meant by database system architecture?

13. Explain the structure of a DBMS.

14. Describe three levels of data abstraction based on the ANSI/SPARC architecture.

15. Write a note on Client/Server DBMS architecture.

16. What is meant by database schema?

17. What is a schema diagram?

18. Describe database schema with an example.

19. What is database state? Give an example.

20. Explain data independence.

References

1. L.B. Bergholt, J.S. Due, R.T. Hohn, J.L. Knudsen, K.H. Nielsen, T.S. Olesen and E.H. Pedersen, "Database Management Systems: Relational, Object-Relational, and Object-Oriented Data models", Center for Object Technology, COT/4-02-V1.1, Pp. 1-120, 1998.

2. T.M. Connolly and C.E. Begg, "Database Systems: A Practical Approach to Design, Implementation, and Management", Fourth Edition, Pearson Education Ltd, 2012.

3. R. Elmasri and S. Navathe, "Database Systems: Models, Languages, Design and Application Programming", Sixth edition, Pearson Education Ltd, 2013.

4. W. Kim, "Object-Relational-The unification of object and relational database technology", UniSQL White Paper, 1996.

5. W. Kim, "Object-Oriented Database Systems: Promises, Reality and Future", Proceedings of the 19th International Conference on Very Large Data Bases, Pp. 676-687, Dublin, Ireland, 1993.

6. S. McClure, "Object Database vs. Object-Relational Databases", International Data Corporation (IDC) Bulletin, 1997.

7. W. Zhang and N. Ritter, "The real benefits of Object-Relational DB-Technology for Object-Oriented Software Development", In Proceedings of the 18th British National Conference on Databases, LNCS 2097, Springer, Pp. 89-104, July 2001.

CHAPTER 3

DATABASE DESIGN AND DEVELOPMENT

Key Features

- Database Development Lifecycle
- Database Design
- Relational Database Systems
- Object-Oriented Database Systems
- Object-Relational Database Systems

3.1. Introduction

Databases and database technology have a major impact on the growing database applications. Database design and development is one of the most important tasks, while following database approach for a reality. The database is an important component of an organization's information system. The development and usage of the database should be viewed from the perspective of the requirements of the organization. Thus, the lifecycle of the organization information system is associated to the database development lifecycle.

Database development is a process of designing a database and implementation. This chapter describes the various stages of the database development lifecycle. The various stages of database development lifecycle include database planning and analysis, database design, database implementation, database testing and maintenance. Database design is one of the important stages in database development lifecycle. A well defined database design is an essential process to meet the requirements of the organization. Database design is the process of creating a design that will support the organization's objectives for the required database system. This chapter discusses the three important phases of database design which include conceptual, logical and physical database design.

The database systems are essential to define the constructs to design and develop databases. A number of database systems are developed based on either record based or object based data models. This chapter presents an overview of three conventional database systems such as relational, object-oriented and object-relational database systems. These database systems implement different data models namely relational, object-oriented and object-relational data models which are used to manage the data with different perfective based on the requirements of advanced applications.

3.2. Database Development Lifecycle

Database system is an important component of an information system (IS) and its development and usage should be viewed from the perspective of the requirements of the organization. Database development is a process of designing a database and implementation. The lifecycle of an organization information system is inherently linked to the database development life cycle.

The various stages of database development life cycle include database planning and analysis, database design, database implementation, database testing and maintenance are shown in Figure 3.1 which is described as follows:

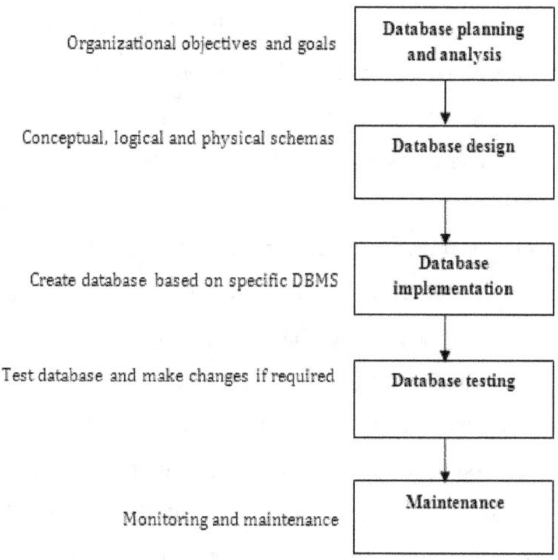

Figure 3.1: Stages of Database Development Life Cycle

- **Database planning and analysis** – Database planning and analysis is the process of collecting and analyzing information based on the organization needs that is to be supported by the database. The various activities performed in this stage are: learn the organization plans and goals, evaluation of current information system to determine existing strengths and weakness, find the sources of information, determine the flow and use of information, documents and reports to be generated, constraints related to the use of information, operational procedures and business policies that are to be applied on information, scope and boundaries of the database system. The outcome of this stage is to develop the database effectively in such a way that it can meet the current and future information requirements of an organization.

- **Database design** – Database design is the process of creating a design that will support the organization's mission objectives for the required database system. Database design involves three phases namely conceptual, logical and physical design of the database.

  - **Conceptual database design** is the process of constructing a conceptual model of the data used in an organization. This design is independent of the database system implementation such as the target DBMS software, programming languages and hardware platform. The main aim of this phase is to build the conceptual representation of the database. The various activities performed in this phase are, identification of entities with their attributes, relationships between entities, specification of candidate and primary key attributes, check model for redundancy, validate the conceptual model against user transactions and review the conceptual data model with user.

  - **Logical database design** is the process of constructing a model of the data used in an organization based on a specific model, but independent of the particular DBMS and other physical considerations. The aim of this phase is to translate the conceptual representation to the logical structure of the database. The various activities performed in this phase are, designing relations for logical model, validate relations using normalization, validate relations against user transactions, check integrity constraints and review logical model with user.

  - **Physical database design** is the process of producing the description of the implementation of the database on secondary storage which includes the file organization, indexes used to achieve efficient access to the data and security measures. This phase decides how the logical structure is physically implemented in the target DBMS. The various activities performed in this phase are, translate logical data model for target DBMS (design base relations, design representation of derived data, design general constraints), design of file organizations and indexes, design user views, design security mechanism, monitor and tune the operational system.

- **Database implementation** – Database implementation is the physical realization of the database. In this stage a database is created as per DBMS software and load the data.

- **Database testing** – Testing is the process of running the database with the intent of checking the database for finding errors.

- **Maintenance** – Maintenance is the process of monitoring and maintaining the system following installation.

3.3.   Database Design

The previous section described the various stages of database development lifecycle and among them database design is the important phase. Database is a repository of business data which is the result of a carefully designed database constructs. Database design is the process of constructing a stable database structure from user requirements analysis. The primary objective of database design is to create complete, normalized and non-redundant fully integrated database system. Hence a well defined database design methodology is an essential one to meet the requirements of the organization. A design methodology uses procedures, techniques, tools and documentation support to facilitate the process of design in a structured manner. A well structured design approach helps the database designer to plan, manage, control and evaluate database development as effectively as possible.

Database Design Process

The accurate and consistent data in the database is essential for organization and thus one need to pay attention to the design of database. A well designed database system requires good database design process. The database design stage starts only after a complete analysis of the organization's requirements. The various phases of database design process as shown in Figure 3.2 are described as the following.

- **Requirements analysis** – The first phase of the database design process is to perform requirement analysis to understand about, the data to be stored in the database, the operations that are to be performed on data and also the applications that are to be built on the top of the database. Several methodologies and automated tools are used for organizing and gathering information. The requirements of a database application are determined through various ways such as interviews with members concerned, reports presently used by the users with related processing requirements and the analysis of available documentation on existing application. The outcome of this phase is to design the database in such a way that it can meet the current and future data requirements based on the organizational goals and objective.

- **Conceptual design** – The second phase of the design process is to design a DBMS independent data model, which gives a stable comprehensive view of the entire database. This phase is carried out using the ER model. The data gathered in the requirements analysis phase is used to develop a high level description of the data to be stored in the database along with constraints. Construction of the ER model gives the diagrammatic representation of the overall conceptual design of the database to describe the data in a real world enterprise in terms of objects called as entities and their relationships.

- **Logical design** – After designing the conceptual data model, it should be mapped into any one of the representational or internal data models such as relational, object-oriented and object-relational to implement DBMS. Selecting the right type of data model is an important task, since it will improve the efficiency of operation of the database system.

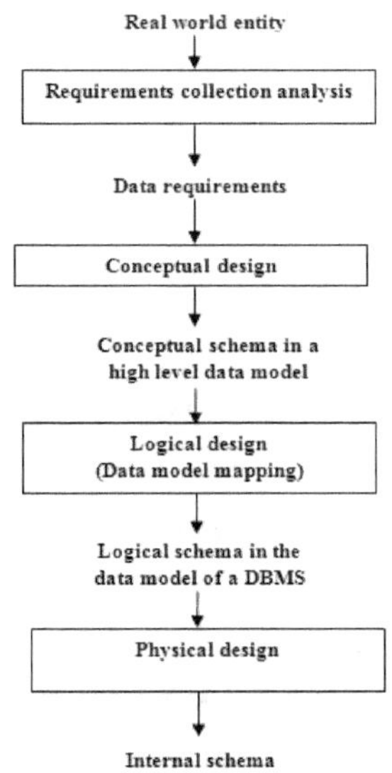

Figure 3.2: Phases of Database Design Process

- **Physical design** – After mapping the data model, the next phase is to design a physical data model. The designing of physical data model decides the various features such as stored record formats, selecting access methods, database security, integrity, backup procedures and recovery methods.

The various characteristics of a good database design process which reduce the development costs of database are the following:

- Iterative requirements analysis – interview top down, use simple models for data flow and data relationships, verify model.
- Stepwise refinement and iterative re-design.

- Well-defined design review process– reviews various teams that include database designers, DBMS software group and end-users in the application areas to clarify their requirements and rectify problems related to database design up-to-date.

Database Design Approaches

The two approaches for designing the database are top-down approach and bottom-up approach. Top-down approach first identifies the entities and their relationships based on the data requirements of an organization. Then the data elements or attributes of each entity are defined. Bottom-up approach first defines the data elements and then groups them together to form entities. The top-down approach is suitable to design a database for large organization with wide scope of operations and the bottom-up approach is employed for small organization with limited scope of operations.

3.4.   Overview of Conventional Database Systems

Database systems are essential to define the constructs and formalisms through a DBMS to define, store, access and maintain the data in databases based on the requirement of user or application programs. Database systems are used to support a variety of tasks and requirements run by applications from business to science.

This section describes the three conventional database systems such as relational, object-oriented and object-relational database systems. These database systems implement different data models namely relational, object-oriented and object-relational data models which are used to manage the data with different perfective based on the requirements of users.

3.4.1.   Relational Database Systems

A relational database system (RDBS) is developed based on the relational model. The only data structure supported by the relational model is the relation which is organized in the form of a two-dimensional table. An element of a relation is called a tuple or record and a relation is a set of tuples. A relation has a name and a well defined structure called a relation schema. A relation schema consists of set of attributes which represents the properties of a real world object called an entity. Each attribute has associated a name which is unique within the relation schema and a scalar domain such as integer, real, string and date.

For example, a relation schema for an employee relation named as Employee Schema is specified as follows.

Employee Schema

R= (<u>EmpID</u>: INTEGER PRIMARY KEY, Name: CHAR (40), Salary: INTEGER, Dept: CHAR (10))

A relational database system consists of tables made up of rows and columns. In the RDBS, tables are created with unique name and each table consists of records corresponds to an application entity. Each row or record represents an instance of that entity and each column has name with single data type. The RDBS supports various data types such as string, numeric and date.

For example, Table 3.1 shows an Employee table which consists of three records. Each record in the table represents an instance of data which describes the attributes of an employee such as employee ID, name, salary and department.

Table 3.1: Employee Table

EmpID	Name	Salary	Department
001	Hari	45000	Information Technology
002	Praveen	40000	Information Technology
003	Ramkumar	25000	Marketing

The relational database system also defines operations which work on relations. A basic set of six operations that are used to express all relational algebra operations are the set union ($\cup$), set difference ($\Leftrightarrow$) and cross product ($\times$) of two relations, selection (σ), projection (π) and rename (β) operations on a single relation. The result of each of these operations is another relation. The set union operation adds all tuples of both relations involved into a single relation. The set difference returns all tuples of the first relation which do not occur in the second. The cross product combines all tuples of the first relation with all tuples of the second relation and the resulting relation contains all attributes of the first and the second relation. Selection returns a subset of rows of a relation and projection returns a subset of columns. The rename operation allows the renaming of attributes in a relation. Other operations can also be expressed by using a combination of these six operations. For example, to find the employee ID and name of the employee those who are earning more than 25000 from Employee table as shown in Table 3.1. This can be expressed by a selection and a projection operation using relational algebra as follows:

$$\pi[\text{EmpID, Name}](\sigma[\text{Salary}>25000] (\text{Employee})) \text{ ----------------------------- (1)}$$

The selection operation first select the tuples in Employee relation whose value in attribute Salary is more than 25000. The resulting relation is projected to a relation containing only the columns EmpID and Name as shown below.

EmpID	Name
001	Hari
002	Praveen

The relational database system supports the structured query language (SQL) which is the standard language for retrieving and manipulating data in relational database systems. The SQL standard was first published in 1986 and significantly enhanced in 1989 (SQL-89). Over the years an improvement and expansion to the SQL standard has continued through the various revisions such as SQL-92 (SQL2), SQL: 1999 (SQL3), SQL: 2003 (SQL4) and SQL: 200n.

The SQL is divided into three parts: data definition language (DDL), data modification language (DML) and the query language. Base tables, indexes and views are created using DDL. A base table is a relation that is physically stored in the database. Indexes are access paths to base tables which allow a faster lookup of specific data in the table. A view is virtual table and it is not physically stored in the database. The DML is used to insert, update and delete data in tables. The query language allows the retrieval of data and also supports various features such as aggregation functions, grouping and ordering of tuples. SQL is a declarative and set-oriented language. SQL queries specify what data is desired, but not how the data is retrieved. The query language compiler translates an SQL statement into low-level operations accessing the data on the storage management level. Optimization is performed to select the most efficient execution of a query.

The relational algebra expression (1), to find the EmpID and Name of the employees those who earning the salary above 25000 are written using SQL is as follows:

SELECT EmpID, Name

FROM   Employee

WHERE Salary > 25000

A RDBS supports several integrity constraints such as primary keys, foreign keys and referential integrity. A primary key is an attribute or set of attributes of relation whose value uniquely identifies a tuple in a relation. For example, in the Employee relation schema R, the attribute EmpID is specified as the primary key. A foreign key is an attribute or a set of attributes of one table that contains only values of the primary key of another referenced table. The referential integrity constraint for a relation demands that each of its foreign key values must exist also a primary key value in the referenced table. In the RDBS relationships among data are expressed using foreign keys and verified using referential integrity constraints.

The relational database system is value based and an entity is identified via primary key. A key is either generated by a program or written by an application program. The same entity can have different keys in different relations. Relational database systems are powerful to support business data processing applications such as inventory control system, payroll system, financial system, and reservation system. The advantages of relational database systems include data independence, multiple views of data and a non-procedural set oriented language that is suitable for atomic query optimization.

Even though relational database systems are effective mechanism for structured data management requirements in large and small organizations, the advanced application areas such as computer-aided design (CAD), computer-aided manufacturing (CAM), computer-aided software engineering (CASE), office information system (OIS), multimedia system, digital publishing, interactive and dynamic websites, scientific and medical applications handle complex object-oriented data which are difficult to represent in relational database systems. Since relational data model supports only structured, predefined data types with simple modeling and not designed to manage arbitrary user-defined data types with complex modeling.

Using a relational database system for an object-oriented application requires, additional processing and complexity for moving objects and mapping complex data into the relational structure. The limitations of the relational database system demand the need for advanced database systems integrated with object-oriented programming system for modeling, storing and manipulating large complex data as well as the object support at the database level.

3.4.2. *Object-Oriented Database Systems*

An Object-oriented database system (OODBS) is developed based on the object-oriented data model that implements the concept of object-oriented programming system (OOPS). OOPS is a paradigm that uses objects, data structures consisting of data fields and methods together with the support of object-oriented concepts. The integration of database systems with OOPS provides an integrated application development environment with many features including the support of objects, methods and classes, abstraction, encapsulation, inheritance, polymorphism, overriding, maintainability, ease of modeling real world objects and database facilities for developing, modifying, and extending complex data intensive software systems. Object-oriented data model provides not only storing complex values but also behaviour in a database, thereby allowing applications to share code as well as data. Object-oriented data models are identity-based. Thus the OODBS allows users for storing and manipulating complex data as well as the object support at the database level.

In OODBS, the data is defined in terms of objects based on identity. An object is referenced via unique system generated number which is called as object identifier (OID). The IOD has no semantics and usually is not visible to the user. The OODBS allows the storage of all information concerning an entity as a single database object. In OODBS, an object consists of an object identifier, its state and behaviour. The state of an object is specified by a data structure of arbitrary complexity. State values of objects are constructed from a combination of simple attributes, reference attributes and complex attributes. Simple attributes contain values of certain atomic data type such as integer, real and string. Reference attributes store the OID of another object and thus an object can comprise other objects. Complex attributes store binary large objects (BLOBS). The behaviour of an object is specified by operations that are called as methods. The code of these methods is stored in the database.

An object is an instance of a class which defines both state and behaviour of the object. All objects in a class share a common definition but differ in the values assigned to their attributes. Association between objects is expressed in two ways. First, a reference to another object is implemented and the OID of the referenced object is stored implicitly within the state of the object. Second, association between objects is specified as explicitly. This database system also provides support for the persistence of objects. An object query language (OQL) is used to fetch an object from the database. The main advantage of using the object-oriented database system is to provide the capabilities for modeling, storing and manipulating complex objects through object-oriented data model.

Object-oriented database systems improve relational database systems by providing object-oriented concepts. The object-oriented database system supports Binary Large Objects (BLOBS) such as images, video, audio and animations. Even though the object-oriented database system is well suited for storing and retrieving complex data and also captures the state as well as behavior of the objects, still it lacks the standard model as known in the relational model. Also the object-oriented database system is not compatible with relational database systems and do not include several relational features such as a complete declarative query language, metadata management, views and authorization.

3.4.3. *Object-Relational Database Systems*

The limitations of relational and object-oriented database systems made database developers generate another type of database system namely object-relational database system (ORDBS) which is developed based on the object-relational data model. The ORDBS unifies the relational database technology with object-oriented programming concepts through both relational and object-oriented data model. Object-relational database systems have the ability to represent complex data as well as the multimedia data and also designed to avoid the impedance mismatch between object-oriented languages and relational database systems.

The ORDBS allows the users to effectively model and manipulate the unstructured data and to use object-oriented concepts for application development without losing the benefits of SQL with all the necessary features of a commercial-strength DBMS. Object-relational database systems have gained acceptance as a powerful technology for handling complex database applications by extending the relational database system with object-oriented features such as user defined data types, functions, reference attributes, inheritance and polymorphism.

Features of ORDBSs

The various features of the object-relational database system are the following:

- Easy to model the complex object structures of advanced applications with enriched object-oriented modeling features.
- Ability to store complex objects persistently and also to enable the stored objects to be shared as a common resource by database applications.
- Support for extensible data types for managing unstructured complex data types such as text, image, audio, and video data. Extensible type system in ORDBS permits to add new application specific data types and functions. The ORDBS venders use different names for extensible type systems e.g. data blades from Informix, extenders from DB2, data cartridges from Oracle.
- A rich type system which allows for defining abstract data types (ADTs), arranging types in inheritance hierarchies, mapping relationships as references and defining complex data types with the help of constructors. ADTs allow new data types with structures suited to particular applications to be defined.
- Ability to create user-defined data types (UDTs), which increases expressiveness and maintainability in object-oriented applications. UDTs provide the means for writing customized server functions.
- Support for smart BLOBS, that are disk based objects that have the functionality of random access files. ADTs use them to store any data that does not fit into a table row.
- An extensible and flexible indexing such as R-tree or Generalized Search Tree (GiST) indexing for multidimensional data enables fast searching of particular ADTs in a table. Traditional B-tree indexing is suitable for data that can be ordered in a one dimension but for multidimensional such as polygons R-tree of GiST index is more suitable.
- Ability to support composite data types which allow data to be bundled together with metadata and queried using SQL. The integration of data and metadata provides various advantages in ORDBS such as improved concurrency and integrity, database extensibility, uniform treatment of data items, point-in-time recovery of data, built-in complex SQL functions, and custom data access methods.

- Support for stored procedures and functions.

- Support for inheritance, a way to define a new data type as specialization of one or more existing types.

- Support for polymorphism, which involves runtime selection of functions based on the dynamic types of their arguments.

- Support for user friendly interaction and consistency control.

- Ability to enable dynamic World Wide Web (WWW) connections.

- Repository functionality called XML native type is used to store XML documents in the database without any conversion and support updates, queries, indexing and views on this type of data.

- Support for complex applications and compatible with RDBMS.

- Support for active mechanisms, allowing users to specify constraints that govern how data are modified and automatic actions called triggers that are executed when certain conditions are detected in the database.

- Flexible and extensible architecture for satisfying the application domain specific needs.

SQL3 standard is characterized as object-oriented SQL and it becomes the foundation for several commercial object-relational database systems. The ORDBS standard SQL3 is a superset of RDBS standard SQL92, which maintains backward compatibility while adding object-oriented features that includes user defined types, methods, references, collections and large objects. Also SQL3 standard provides support for active rules in object-relational database systems. The SQL4 standard has also been published which makes revisions to SQL3 with enriched object-relational model.

The object-relational database system provides declarative object-oriented query language for defining, accessing and updating objects. Object classes are defined as types and object attributes and methods are defined as functions. The ORDBS supports various data types such as alphanumeric data, simple large objects, abstract data types, user-defined data types, objects, classes, inheritance, user-defined routines and user-defined access methods. ORDBSs provide an object-oriented front-end on a relational database. When applications interact with this database, they interact normally as if the data is stored as objects. However, at the back-end, the system converts the objects into tables and manipulates the data as like in a relational database system. Also after manipulation, the data is converted into objects and returned to the application. Thus the object-relational database system requires software to convert the object data between an object-oriented format and the relational database format interchangeably.

The main advantage of using an object-relational database system is the support of defining new data types through user-defined routines that help in storing, accessing and managing objects and large text documents. However the performance of this database system is little bit slower in terms of speed, since the object-relational database system converts data between object-oriented format and the relational format interchangeably.

3.5. Summary

This chapter has explained the concept of database system design and development. Database development is viewed as a process of designing a database and implementation. In this chapter, the various stages of the database development lifecycle include database planning and analysis, database design, database implementation, database testing and maintenance are presented. A well structured design approach helps the database designer to plan, manage, control and evaluate database development as effectively as possible. This chapter has described the three phases of database design process which include conceptual, logical and physical database design. This chapter has explained the three types of database systems such as the relational, object-oriented and object-relational database systems which are used to store and manage the data with different perfective based on the requirements of database applications.

Review Questions

1. What is meant by database development?
2. Explain the various stages of database development lifecycle.
3. What is meant by database testing and maintenance?
4. What is database design?
5. Describe the different phases of database design process.
6. What are the two approaches used to design a database?
7. Explain relational database systems.
8. Write the limitations of relational database systems.
9. Explain object-oriented database systems.
10. What are the advantages of object-oriented database systems?
11. Explain object-relational database systems.
12. Write the advantages of object-relational database systems.

References

1. S. Bagui, "Achievements and Weaknesses of Object-Oriented Databases", Journal of Object Technology, Vol. 2, No. 4, Pp. 29-41, 2003.

2. H. Butuner, "Advantages of Object-Oriented Over Relational Databases on Real-Life Applications", Research Journal of Economics, Business and ICT, ISSN: 2045-3345, Vol. 5, 2012.

3. T.M. Connolly and C.E. Begg, "Database Systems: A Practical Approach to Design, Implementation, and Management", Fourth Edition, Pearson Education Ltd, 2012.

4. R.S. Devarkonda, "Object-relational Database Systems-the road ahead", ACM Crossroads, Vol. 7, No. 3, Pp. 15-18, 2001.

5. A. Eisenberg and J. Melton, "SQL: 1999, formerly known as SQL3", SIGMOD Record, Vol. 28, No. 1, Pp. 131-138, 1999.

6. R. Elmasri and S. Navathe, "Database Systems: Models, Languages, Design and Application Programming", Sixth edition, Pearson Education Ltd, 2013.

7. M. Jackson, "Thirty years (and more) of databases", Information and Software Technology, Elsevier, Vol. 41, No. 14, Pp. 969-978, 1999.

8. W. Kim, "Object-Relational - The unification of object and relational database technology", UniSQL White Paper, 1996.

9. W. Kim, "Object-Oriented Database Systems: Promises, Reality and Future", In Proceedings of the 19th International Conference on Very Large Data Bases, Pp. 676-687, Dublin, Ireland, 1993.

10. S. McClure, "Object Database vs. Object-Relational Databases", International Data Corporation (IDC) Bulletin, 1997.

11. W. Zhang and N. Ritter, "The real benefits of Object-Relational DB-Technology for Object-Oriented Software Development", In Proceedings of the 18th British National Conference on Databases, LNCS 2097, Springer, Pp. 89-104, 2001.

CHAPTER 4

TRANSACTION MANAGEMENT IN DATABASE SYSTEMS

Key Features

- Transaction Concepts
- Transaction Execution
- Classification of Transactions
- Correctness Criteria for Transactions
- Concurrency Control Algorithms
- Transaction Models

4.1.   Introduction

Database management systems are largely concerned with the problems of performance, correctness, maintainability, and reliability. A major concern for a database system is the notion of correctness and the correctness of the database is ensured by means of transactions execution. The main goal of transaction management is to guarantee the correctness of the database while performing the two closely related DBMS functions namely transaction support and concurrency control. A system that manages transactions and controls their access to a DBMS is called the transaction manager that coordinates transactions on behalf application programs and it communicates with the scheduler which is responsible for controlling concurrent execution of transactions by implementing a specific algorithm for concurrency control. Thus, transaction manager and scheduler are the two important components of the DBMS to carry out the transaction processing in database systems.

This chapter presents the transaction concept which includes transaction states, transaction execution and transaction classification. The various states of transaction during its execution are: begin, commit, abort and end. The four basic properties of a transaction include atomicity, consistency, isolation and durability (ACID) properties which are used to ensure the database stable state after the transaction is executed. The transactions are classified based on the two factors such as duration and structure for effective transaction processing in database systems.

When a database is shared and updated by multiple transactions concurrently, a correctness criterion is needed to ensure the correctness of the database. This chapter discusses the various correctness criteria which include serializability and non-serializability for defining the correctness of transaction execution in database systems. In general, serializability is the most widely accepted correctness criterion for controlling the order of concurrent execution of transactions and is achieved through various concurrency control algorithms.

This chapter explains the concurrency control algorithms to ensure the correctness of the database system. Several problems such as last update, temporary update, and incorrect summary can occur when concurrent transactions are executed in an uncontrolled manner. Thus every multiuser DBMS needs certain concurrency control algorithm to protect the correctness of its data. The scheduler component implements concurrency control algorithm which is also referred to as lock manager, if the concurrency control algorithm is locking.

When several transactions are executed concurrently, transaction models provide mechanism to solve many of the problems incurred by concurrent access to shared data in large databases. A transaction model is basically a set of rules which govern the execution and properties of transactions. This chapter also discusses the various types of transaction models used for transaction processing in database systems.

4.2. Transaction Concepts

A database consists of a finite set of data entities which are shared by many users who update the database with transactions. A transaction is defined as an action that is carried out by a single user or application program to perform operations for accessing the contents of the database. A transaction is a program unit whose execution may change the contents of the database and its execution should preserve the consistency of the database. A transaction is a sequence of READ and WRITE actions that are grouped together to form a database access. A transaction which successfully completes its execution is said to be committed and all its changes must be recoded permanently in the database. A transaction is aborted when the transaction detects an error during its execution and those transactions are rolled back to undo the effect its operation. The various states of transaction during its execution are: begin, commit, abort and end. Thus transactions provide mechanism for organizing and synchronizing database operations.

Transaction Execution

Transactions are executed by a database system in such a way that either all operations are executed or in the case of system failure or inconsistency, none of them are executed, i.e., transactions are atomic. Also if multiple users or applications operate on the same database, transactions are serializable. A transaction that executed and terminated normally is referred to as committed transaction, while a transaction that did not finish normally, regardless of the failure is said to be aborted. In database systems, transactions have four basic properties called as ACID (Atomicity, Consistency, Isolation and Durability) properties which are used to ensure that a database remains stable state after the transaction is executed. The atomicity and durability property is the responsibility of the recovery subsystem of the DBMS. The preservation of consistency is the responsibility of the DBMS and integrity and enterprise constraints are enforced by the application developers. The isolation property is enforced by the concurrency subsystem of the DBMS.

The two types of transaction execution supported by the DBMS are serial and concurrent execution. The transactions that execute one by one sequentially are called as serial execution. Two or more transactions that execute at a time in an interleaved manner are called as concurrent execution. The serial execution of transactions is suitable for single-user DBMS. When a database is shared and updated by multiple users at a time, concurrent execution of transactions is necessary to improve the system performance. Thus multiuser DBMS requires concurrent execution of transactions.

Classification of Transactions

In general transactions are classified based on the two factors such as duration and structure for effective transaction processing in database applications. Based on duration, a transaction is classified as short duration and long duration transactions. Short duration transactions are characterized by short execution times in seconds and by competitive access to a small portion of the database. Long duration transactions are characterized by longer execution times in minutes/hours and cooperative access to a larger portion of the database. Based on the structure, a transaction is classified as single level and multilevel transaction. A transaction which is not decomposable is called as single level structure and it completely runs in isolation that commits or fails. If the transaction fails, all the changes made on the database state are undone. The division of complex transactions into sub transactions according to the semantic of applications is called as multilevel structure of transactions.

4.3.   Correctness Criteria for Transactions

A major concern for database system is the notion of correctness and the correctness of the database is ensured by means of transactions. Transactions operating on a database system have to take the database from one correct database state to another and are accomplished by preserving ACID properties. In general, transactions comply with ACID properties are execute transactions serially one after the other.

Even though serial executions are correct because transactions that execute serially cannot interfere with each other, it may result in small transaction throughput with long response time to process transactions. Since this is too restrictive, a concurrent (interleaved) execution of transactions is expected to have the same effect of serial transaction that is referred to as serializable execution. Even if individual transactions are correct, transactions can interfere with each other when they are executed concurrently thereby producing inconsistent results. Therefore the interleaved execution of a set of transactions is controlled by providing the necessary isolation between concurrent transactions to execute without any interference in operating on a consistent database. In order to ensure the correctness of serializable execution of transactions, concurrency control algorithms are required in database systems.

Criteria for Defining the Correctness of the Database

The two criteria for defining the correctness of the database are database integrity and serializability. The database integrity is satisfied by assigning a set of constraints that must be satisfied for a database to correct. The serializability ensures that database transitions from one state to other are based on an interleaved execution of a set of concurrent transactions. In general serializability is used as a correctness criterion for concurrency control in database applications and it requires that the execution of each transaction cannot be interrupted by other transactions. Hence to maintain serializability based correctness, the database system through scheduler has to produce a schedule of concurrent execution of a set of transactions is equivalent to a serial execution of a set of transactions represented by a serial schedule. Serializability based correctness criteria are the elegant way of verifying both the data consistency and transaction scheduling correctness requirements. Serializability support only flat transactions that can perform atomic database operations. Serializability in database systems is guaranteed through the designing of concurrency control algorithms.

Limitations of Serializability Based Correctness Criteria

While serializability is successfully used in traditional applications that are characterized by short duration transactions with competitive access to shared data, it is restrictive and hardly applicable in nontraditional applications characterized by long duration transactions with cooperative access to shared data since it prevents a transaction from seeing the intermediate results of another transaction.

Serializability is appropriate when no information is known about the transactions submitted to the DBMS. However advanced applications have semantic information that should be employed when maintaining the consistency of the data. The semantic information refers to any important knowledge about transaction, its operations or its relationships with other transactions.

Requirement of Non-Serializable Correctness Criteria

The limitations of serializability are improved by the introduction of various non-serializable correctness criteria that extends traditional serializability to serve the different application requirements. The various flexible or non-serializable correctness criteria are described as the following:

- **Cooperative Serializability (COSR)** is an alternative correctness criterion for cooperative databases and it is defined with respect to a set of transactions which maintain the consistency properties. Transactions form cooperative transaction sets and a cooperative transaction set could be formed by the components of an extended transaction or transactions collaborating over the objects while maintaining the consistency of the objects. In such cases, consistency can be maintained if other transactions which do not belong to the set are serialized with respect to all the transactions in the set. In other words, a set of cooperative transactions becomes the unit of concurrency with respect to serializability.

- **Epsilon-Serializability (ESR)** is introduced as a generalization of serializability where a limited amount of inconsistency is permitted and the concurrency is enhanced by permitting the non-serializable schedules. ESR defines correctness for both consistent and inconsistent database states. ESR introduces the notion of epsilon transactions (ETs) by attaching a specification of the amount of permitted inconsistency to each transaction. ESR aims at bounding the amount of imported and exported inconsistency for each ET. ESR distinguishes between transactions that contain only read operation, called query epsilon transaction and transactions with at least one update operation called update epsilon transaction. Query ETs may view uncommitted, possibly inconsistent, data being updated by update ETs. Thus updates ETs are seen as exporting the inconsistencies while query ETs are importing these inconsistencies.

- **Eventual Consistency** is an alternative correctness criterion for distributed databases with replicated or interdependent data. A correctness criterion that ensures eventual consistencies is the current copy **serializability**. Each update occurs on a current copy and is asynchronously propagated to other replicas. Eventual consistency requires that duplicate copies are consistent at certain times but may be inconsistent in the interim intervals. The basic idea is that duplicates are allowed to diverge as long as the copies are made consistent periodically. The times where these copies are made consistent could depend on the application.

- **Multiversion Serializability (MVS)** in multiversion databases each write on a data item 'x'produces a new version (or copy) of 'x'. For each read on 'x' the database selects one of the versions of 'x' to be read and write do not overwrite each other and since reads can read any version of the database. Hence concurrency is increased by having transactions read older versions while other concurrent transactions are creating newer versions. In a multi version database only one type of conflict is possible; when a transaction reads a version of a data item that **was** written by another transaction. Based on the assumption that users expect their transactions to behave as if there were just one copy of each data item, the notion of one-copy serial schedule is defined. A schedule is one-copy serial (1-serial) if for all i, j, and x, if a transaction Tj reads 'x' from a transaction Ti, then either i = j or Ti is the last transaction preceding Tj that writes into any version of 'x'. Hence a schedule is defined as one copy serializability (1-SR) if it is equivalent to a 1-serial schedule.

- **Predicate wise Serializability (PWSR)** is a correctness criterion for long duration transaction processing environments such as CAD and Office information systems. PWSR focus on database consistency constraints that can be expressed in conjunctive normal form. If database consistency constraints are expressed in a conjunctive normal form, a schedule is said to be PWSR if all projections of that schedule on each group of data items that share a disjunctive clause are serializable. The restrictions that must be enforced on PWSR schedules to preserve database consistency are: force the transactions to be of fixed structure, i.e., they are independent of the database state from which they execute, force the schedules to be delayed read, i.e., a transaction Ti cannot read a data item written by a transaction T_j until after T_j has completed all of its operations, and the conjuncts of the integrity constraints can be ordered in a way that no transaction reads a data item belonging to a higher numbered conjunct and writes a data item belonging to a lower numbered conjunct.

- **Quasi Serializability (QSR)** is a correctness criterion for global concurrency control in heterogeneous distributed database system (HDDBS). HDDBS consists of a set of local databases (LDBSs) and a set of local and global transactions: Local transactions that access only one LDBS and global transactions that access more than one LDBS. A global schedule in an HDDBS is a set of local schedules where the local schedule is defined over global and local transactions. The basic idea of QSR is that in order to preserve global database consistency, global transactions should be executed in a serializable way with proper consideration of the effects of local transactions. A quasi serial schedule is a schedule where global transactions are required to execute serially and local schedules are required to be serializable. A global schedule in an HDDBS is said to be quasi serializable if it is (conflict) equivalent to a quasi serial schedule.

- **Relative Serializability(RSR)** is introduced as a correctness criterion for collaborative databases. RSR introduces the notion of relative atomicity of coactions as a relaxation of the traditional atomicity property. It is used to specify how coactions are interleaved relative to other coactions without breaking the overall atomicity requirement for the collaboration activity. The main idea is that before a collaborative activity takes place first a collaborative channel is established and then correctness is checked against RSR. That is any execution obeying the RSR criterion would preserve the consistency of the database even it is not serializable.

- **Semantic Serializability** is an approach for controlling concurrency that exploits the semantic information available about transactions to allow controlled non-serializable interleaving. The semantic information about transaction takes the form of transaction types, transaction steps and transaction break points. An approach used to define the notion of consistency called relative consistency (RC) that describes the action of allowable interleaving among transactions that known to be correct and also to ensure that each schedule produced by the system is equivalent to a correct schedule. Enforcing relative consistency requires knowledge about the application which must be provided by the user and the transaction failure can be handled by using the method of counter steps. In particular, users will need to group actions of the transactions into steps and specify which steps of a transaction of a given type can be interleaved with the steps of another type of transactions without violating consistency.

- **Two-level Serializability (2LSR)** is a correctness criterion for multi database system (MDBS) to relax serializability requirements and allow higher degree of concurrency. The MDBS consists of set of heterogeneous autonomous pre existing local databases and a set of local and global transactions. 2LSR schedules preserve consistency by exploiting the nature of integrity constraints and transactions in multi database environments. A global schedule consisting of both local and global transactions is

2LSR if all local schedules are serializable and the projection of that schedule on global transactions is serializable. Local schedules consist of all operations, from global and local transactions, that access the same local database.

The universally accepted correctness criterion for processing transactions against a database is serializability and it is achieved through various concurrency control algorithms. The objective of concurrency control protocol is to schedule transactions in such a way to avoid any interference between them and also to correctly process transactions that are in conflict.

4.4.   Concurrency Control Algorithms

An important objective for developing a database is to enable users to access shared data concurrently. When a database is shared and updated by multiple transactions concurrently, concurrency control is needed to ensure the correctness of the database. Concurrency control algorithms are used to ensure serializable execution of transactions. A main concern in designing a concurrency control algorithm is to schedule transactions in such a way to avoid any interference between them and also to correctly process transactions that are in a conflict. Each transaction has a read set and a write set. Two transactions conflict if the read set of one transaction intersects with the write set of the other transaction and/or the write set of one transaction conflicts with the write set of the other transaction. For example T1 and T2 can conflict, only if both are executing at the same time. If T1 has finished before T2 was submitted to the system, even if their read and write sets intersect, they are not considered to be in conflict.

A DBMS employs a concurrency control mechanism, to guarantee consistency of its data as multiple transactions execute concurrently. Thus a concurrency control protocol defines set of rules that allow the system to concurrently execute transactions preserving the desired properties.

Basic Concurrency Control Techniques

The three basic generic techniques used to design the concurrency control algorithms are locking, timestamp ordering (pessimistic) and optimistic. Pessimistic approaches cause transactions to be delayed (wait or rollback) in case they conflict with other transactions at some time in the future. Optimistic methods are based on the premise that conflict is rare so they allow transactions to continue unsynchronized and only check for conflicts at the end when a transaction commits.

Based on the above approaches the five main concurrency control algorithms proposed are two-phase locking (2PL), multi granularity locking, timestamp ordering, multiversion timestamp ordering and optimistic concurrency control.

- ***Locking Methods***

Locking methods are the most widely used approach to ensure serializability of concurrent transactions and it is used to solve the problem of synchronizing access to shared data. The idea behind locking is: each data item has a lock associated with it. Before a transaction T_1 may access a data item, the scheduler first examines the associated lock. If no transaction holds the lock, then the scheduler obtains the lock on behalf of T_1. Suppose if another transaction T_2 does hold the lock, then T_1 has to wait until T_2 gives up the lock. That is, the scheduler will not give T_1 the lock until T_2 releases it. The scheduler there by ensures that only one transaction can hold the lock at a time, thus only one transaction can access the data item at a time. Locking methods generally prevent conflicts by making transactions wait.

Two-phase locking (2PL) is the most commonly implemented concurrency control algorithm in commercial database systems for guarantying serializability of schedules. In 2PL method, each transaction is divided into two phases: a growing phase during which it obtains all the locks needed and cannot release any locks, and a shrinking phase during which it releases locks and cannot acquire any new locks. When a transaction requests a lock it moves into its growing phase and once an unlock request occurs, the transaction moves into shrinking phase. There are two kinds of lock methods, shared and excusive. Multiple transactions can obtain the same shared lock. If a transaction T holds an exclusive lock for A, no other transaction can obtain a shared/exclusive lock on A. The three modes of operation are, read, write and update. Update lock mode indicates a read-write operation, which means current operation of a transaction is reading the item, and the transaction modifies the item in later operation. Lock conflicts, if more than two transactions are accessing same shared data and are solved by making the lock requester wait for the holder of the lock in a FCFS (First-Come-First-Served) queue.

Locking protocols which block transactions on conflict are subject to deadlock. Deadlock occurs when a transaction T in a set of two or more transactions is waiting for an item locked by another transaction T' in the set. In these cases further mechanisms are needed to avoid deadlock. The three techniques for handling deadlock are: timeouts, deadlock prevention, and deadlock detection and recovery. A widely used method is based on timeouts, i.e. a transaction which experiences a conflict can waits at most for a system-defined period of time, after which it gets aborted. This is a low cost method, but it can cause the abort of a transaction. The method based on timeouts is the simple and practical solution to deadlock prevention and is used by several commercial DBMS.

In Deadlock prevention method, transactions are ordered using timestamps based on wait-die and wound-wait approaches. Wait-die, allows only an older transaction to wait for a younger one, otherwise the transaction is aborted and restarted with the same timestamp that will become the oldest active transaction and will not die. Wound-wait, uses only a younger transaction can wait for an older one. If older transaction requests a lock held by a younger one, the younger one is aborted.

Deadlock detection is based on the construction of a wait-for graph (WFG). WFG is a directed graph that indicates which transactions are waiting for which other transactions. Nodes of the graph represent the transactions and the resources held by the transactions, and edges represent the waiting-for relationship.

In a directed graph, where a node 'i' corresponds to a transaction T_i and an edge from a node i to a node j means that the transaction T_i is blocked due to a lock held by a transaction T_j. When a lock conflict occurs the corresponding edge is added to the graph. A cycle in the graph indicates that the deadlock has occurred and it is solved by aborting a transaction in the cycle. The aborted transaction has to be subsequently restarted. The drawback of WFG method is due to the graph management cost.

- ### *Timestamp Ordering*

Timestamp ordering concurrency control is a non-lock concurrency control method to handle transactions using timestamps. Transactions are executed in such a way that their execution is equivalent to a serial execution in timestamp order. In a timestamp based concurrency control algorithms, unique timestamps are assigned to transactions by using the system clock at the transaction start time or by incrementing a logical counter every time a new transaction starts. The timestamps of transactions are used in ordering the transactions in accessing data.

Every data item of the database is associated with two timestamps such as a read timestamp which is the timestamp of the last transaction that read that item and a write timestamp which is the timestamp of the last transaction that wrote that data item. If a transaction attempts to read a data item with a higher write timestamp than its timestamp, or tries to write a data item which has higher read timestamp, then the transaction is aborted. If the transaction tries to write a data item with a lower read timestamp and a higher write timestamp, operation is skipped and nothing is done. Otherwise the operation is done and the read or write timestamp of the data item is changed to the transaction's timestamp according to the operation.

Thus with timestamp methods, transactions involved in conflicts are rolled back and restarted without waiting. Timestamp based algorithms are deadlock free but it is prone to restart transactions.

- ***Optimistic Concurrency Control***

Optimistic concurrency control is based on the assumption that database transactions mostly do not conflict with other transactions. There are three phases in optimistic concurrency control:

- Read - Transaction executes, reading values, writing to private storage.
- Validation - When transaction commits, the database checks if the transaction could have possibly conflicted with any other concurrent transaction. If there is a possibility, the transaction aborts and restarted.
- Write - If there is no possibility of conflict, the transaction commits.

Optimistic concurrency control allows any conflicting access without blocking. As soon as transactions finish their work, it goes through a validation process. If a transaction does not involve any inconsistencies, then it is allowed to commit its results and terminate. Otherwise the transaction is aborted and restarted.

If there are few conflicts, validation can be done effectively, and leads to better performance than any other concurrency control methods. However if there are many conflicts, the cost of repeatedly restarting transactions degrade the performance significantly. Optimistic concurrency control is an efficient technique under the cases such as: all transactions are readers, lots of transactions each accessing/modifying only a small amount of data, fraction of transaction execution in which conflicts really take place is small compared to total path length.

4.5. Transaction Models

Transaction models provide mechanism to solve many of the problems incurred by concurrent access to shared data in large databases. A transaction model is basically a set of rules which govern the execution and properties of transactions. Transaction models are used to provide reliable and secure transaction processing in DBMS. Transactions adhering to the ACID properties are guaranteed to be atomic and serializable that is suitable for database applications characterized by short duration transactions and competitive access to shared data.

The advanced applications characterized by long duration with cooperative transactions require the need for extended/advanced transaction models. Advanced transaction models provide solutions for many problems such as correctness, consistency and reliability in transaction processing and database management environments.

Types of Transaction Models

The various types of transaction models used for transaction processing in database systems are described as follows:

- ### *Flat Transaction Model*

Transactions that have strict ACID properties with single level structure is called flat transaction model. Flat transaction is not decomposable that either completely runs in isolation and commits or fails and undoes all the changes made on the way. Flat transaction model process transaction operations sequentially and either the whole transaction is executed completely or it has no effect on the database. Thus when a transaction fails, flat model provides rollback of the entire transaction. The flat transaction model is simple and secure and suitable for applications running with short duration transactions handling simple data. This model is not suitable for applications running with long duration transactions handling complex data as well as in need of cooperation with other transactions. The limitation of flat transaction model provides the proposal of extended/advanced transaction models that relax the ACID properties to better model the parallelism, consistency and serializability requirements of non-traditional applications.

- ### *Extended/Advanced Transaction Models*

In order to overcome the limitations of flat transaction model, the various extended transaction models are proposed. The extended transaction models support relaxed correctness criterion and use relaxed ACID properties for concurrent execution of transactions. The various extended transaction models are described as the following.

- **Nested transaction model** extends the flat transaction model to provide the ability to define transactions within other transactions by splitting a transaction into hierarchies of subtransactions. Nested transaction model is a set of subtransactions that may recursively contain other subtransactions forming the complete transaction tree or hierarchy of transactions. The top level transaction can have number of child transactions and each child transaction can also have nested transactions. A child transaction may start after its parent has started, and may commit locally. The committed local result is, however, released only when all of its parents up to the root have successfully terminated. Transactions have to commit from the bottom upwards and a transaction abort at one level does not have to affect a transaction in progress at a higher level. Hence this model is also termed as closed nested transaction. This model is not appropriate for systems that consist of long transactions and it does not address cooperation since full local and global isolation is required. However, this model allows increased modularity, finer granularity of failure handling and higher intra transaction concurrency than the flat transaction model.

- **Open nested transaction model** is proposed to improve the nested transaction model, to relax the isolation requirements by making the results of committed subtransactions visible to other concurrently executing nested transactions. To avoid inconsistent use of the results of committed subtransactions, only those subtransactions that commute with the committed ones are allowed to use their results. Two transactions are said to commute if their effects, their output and final state of the database are the same regardless of the order in which they were executed. This model also relax the condition of commit process occur in a bottom up fashion through the top level transaction as the semantics of these transactions enforce atomicity at the top level. Hence this model permits higher degree of concurrency and cooperation than the nested transaction model and is suitable for systems that consist of long running with cooperative transactions.

- **Multilevel transaction model** are more generalized versions of nested transactions. Subtransactions of a multilevel transaction can commit and release resources before the global transaction successfully completes and commits. If a global transaction aborts its failure atomicity may require that the effects of already committed subtransactions be undone by executing compensating subtransactions. A compensating transaction T' semantically undoes effects of a committed subtransaction T, so that the state of the database before and after executing a sequence TT' is the same. However, an inconsistency may occur if other transaction S observes the effects of subtransactions that will be compensated later. Open nested transactions use the commutative to solve this problem.

- **Sagas and Nested Sagas** are the transaction models for long-lived activities. A saga consists of a set of ACID transactions $T_1, T_2,...,T_n$ with a predefined order of execution, and a set of compensating subtransactions $CT_1, CT_2,..,CT_{n-1}$, corresponding to $T_1, T_2...T_{n-1}$. A saga completes successfully, if the subtransactions have committed. If one of the subtransactions, say T_k fails, then committed subtransactions $T_{1...}T_{k-1}$ are undone by executing compensating subtransactions $CT_{k-1},...CT_1$. Each subtransaction is allowed to commit individually. A compensating transaction is then used to explicitly undo its effect if the whole Saga transaction has to abort. By allowing subtransactions to commit, thus revealing their partial result(s), Saga relaxes the full isolation requirement and increase inter-transaction concurrency. Hence some degree of cooperation is permitted. The sagas model is further extended as a model called Nested Sagas that provide useful mechanisms to structure steps involved within long running transaction into hierarchical transaction structures. This model promotes a relaxed notion of atomicity whereby forward recovery is used in the form of compensating transactions to undo the effects of a failed transaction.

- **ConTract model** provides a generalized control mechanism for long-lived activities and is aimed at the problem domain of large distributed applications. The basic idea behind this model is to build large applications from short ACID transactions and to provide an application independent system service, which exercises control over them. Also this model does not extend the ACID transactions in structure but embeds them in the application environment and provides reliable execution control over them. In this model a unit of work is defined as a step which ensures the ACID properties but preserves only local consistency. These steps are executed according to a script, which is an explicit control flow description. A reliable and correct execution of the steps is called a ConTract. Hence this model offers control mechanisms like semantic synchronization, context management and compensation at the script level to provide transaction support to a long-lived and complex application.

- **Split/Join transaction model** is designed to provide transactions they have ability to share resources by allowing dynamic reconstruction of running transactions. It is suitable for activities with uncertain duration, unpredictable developments, and interaction with other activities. The basic aim of this model is to split a running transaction into two or more transactions and later join other transactions by merging their resources. Also this model allows cooperation among users by allowing transfer of resources from one transaction to other transactions. Further, it uses an adaptive recovery mechanism which allows part of the work done to be recoverable, and since a committing transaction part may release some of its resources, isolation may somehow be reduced. The main drawback of this model is complex merging mechanisms. Also the two resulting transactions from the split command have to obey a serializability criterion which implies that the two transactions must be seen as two isolated transactions while running.

- **Flex transaction model** is a transaction model for flexible transaction processing in multidatabase systems. A flex transaction is a set of tasks with a set of functionally equivalent subtransactions for each and a set of execution dependencies on the subtransactions including failure dependencies, success dependencies and external dependencies. Flex transaction model relaxes the atomicity and isolation properties of transactions to provide users increased flexibility in specifying their transactions. To relax the isolation requirement, a flexible transaction uses compensation and relaxes global atomicity requirement allows the transaction designer to specify the acceptable states for termination of the flexible transaction. However scalability and access control are not addressed in flexible transaction.

- **Cooperative transaction hierarchy** is a transaction model for design environments and it is a tree based approach similarly like the nested transaction model. The three restricted main levels of this model are: a root, one or more transaction groups and several cooperative transactions. The cooperative transactions correspond to the leaf nodes, which are grouped into transaction groups. They are associated each with a designer in the environment and can, within a transaction group, cooperate on some task. Cooperative transactions are non-serializable and hence for each transaction group, patterns, being a set of rules for how operations can be interleaved, and conflicts, being a set of rules that specify which operations are not allowed to run concurrently, are used as correctness criteria. Although cooperative transaction hierarchy addresses cooperation, its main weakness is the need to define both patterns and conflicts in advance. Hence this model is suitable for applications with a well-defined work structure.

- **Cooperative Activity (CoAct) model** provides the transactional properties applicable to cooperative scenarios. Each user in CoAct works in an own workspace called private workspace and they cooperate through the controlled information exchange and synchronization of their private workspaces. This model works in the following way: a certain parameterized CoAct is used to describe a particular activity and by instantiating it user get a concrete activity. Each participant of a cooperative activity has his/her own activity called user activity and the final result is obtained by merging the result of each user activity. This model is well suited for building asynchronous cooperative applications. But because of the static description of cooperative activity, this model is not flexible enough for advanced cooperative applications.

- **COO** model is developed based on the software development processes requirements with relaxed atomicity and relaxed isolation. Relaxing the atomicity property allows that long transactions may save their intermediate results, thus minimizing losses in the case of crashes and relaxed isolation allows several software processes to access the intermediate results without violating the correctness criterion. In this model intermediate results are managed by applying three different object consistency levels such as stable, semi-stable, and unstable. An object is stable when it is fully consistent i.e., a result from a successfully committed transaction. Semi-stable objects are the processes may generate as tentative data, and can be seen as consistent enough, but may violate the correctness criteria. That is, only processes that satisfy the semantic rules and integrity constraints encoded in the software process description are allowed to use semi-stable objects. Unstable objects are those that do not satisfy the correctness criterion at all, and are currently locked by the processes. This object is inaccessible until it becomes stable or semi-stable objects.

Characterization and Evaluation of Transaction Models

Transaction models are characterized by transaction structure, object structure on which the transactions operate and correctness criterion. The characterization of transaction models is shown in Figure 4.1.

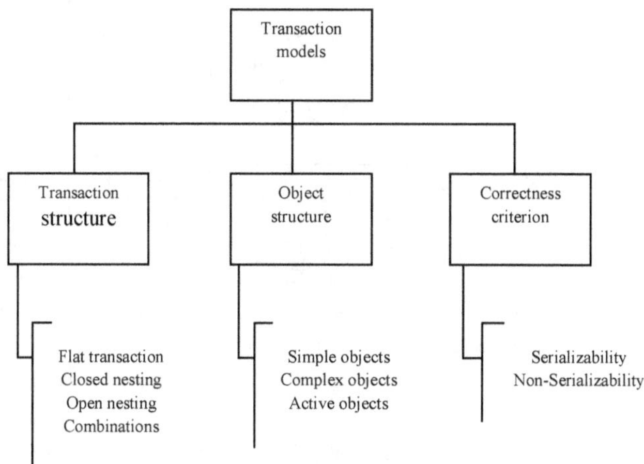

Figure 4.1: Characterization of Transaction Models

The transaction models are evaluated based on the various factors that include transaction properties, transaction structure, intra transaction concurrency, transaction support and the area of application and is shown in Table 4.1. The transaction models specified in Table 4.1 are the various extensions to flat transactions that relax the atomicity and isolation properties with the extension of single level structure (flat) to multi level structures.

Table 4.1: Evaluation of Transaction Models

Transaction Model	Transaction properties	Intra Transaction Concurrency	Transaction structure	Transaction support	Application area
Flat	ACID	No	No internal structure	Short duration transactions	Applications with competitive access to shared data
Nesting	ACID	Yes	Hierarchy of subtransactions	Short duration transactions	Applications with competitive access to shared data
Open nesting and Multilevel	$A^R CI^R D$	Yes	Hierarchy of subtransactions	Short and Long duration transactions	Applications with competitive and cooperative access to shared data
Sagas and Nested Sagas	$ACI^R D$	Yes	Sequence of sub transactions with compensating transactions	Long duration transactions	Applications with cooperative access to data
Contract	ACID	No	Hierarchy of subtransactions	Long duration and complex transactions	Distributed applications
Split/Join	$ACI^R D$	No	Transactions with dynamic reconstruction	Cooperative transactions	Applications with uncertain duration and interaction with Transactions
Flex	$A^R CI^R D$	Yes	Subtransactions with compensating transactions	Cooperative transactions	Multi database environment
Cooperative transaction hierarchy	-	No	Three level tree based approach	Cooperative transactions	Design applications
CoAct	$ACI^R D$	No	Transactions with compensation, dynamic reconstruction	Cooperative transactions	Asynchronous cooperative applications
Coo	$A^R CI^R D$	Yes	Check in and checkout model	Long and cooperative transactions	Software development process

A^R – Relaxed Atomicity – long transactions may save their intermediate results.

I^R – Relaxed Isolation – allows transactions to access intermediate results without violating correctness criteria.

According to transaction structure, the models use two strategies to achieve different structures inside a transaction: (i) modularize a complex transaction with hierarchies. i.e., a large transaction is divided into smaller components, which can in turn be decomposed and this strategy is applied in nested transactions, flexible transactions, and open nested transactions (ii) decomposing a long lasting transaction into shorter subtransactions which include a compensation mechanism and this strategy is applied in sagas, multi level transactions. The specified models support both serializable and non-serializable correctness criteria. Along the object structure dimension the above transaction models operate on simple objects.

4.6. Summary

This chapter has discussed the role of transaction management mechanism in database systems. In this chapter, the transaction concept which includes transaction states, transaction execution and transaction classification are presented. The various correctness criteria which include serializability and non-serializability are discussed for defining the correctness of transaction execution in database systems. This chapter has explained the concurrency control algorithms to ensure the correctness for processing concurrent transactions in the database system. The three basic generic techniques used to design concurrency control algorithms are locking, timestamp ordering (pessimistic) and optimistic. This chapter has also described the various types of transaction models used for secure transaction processing in database systems. Transaction models provide mechanism to solve many of the problems incurred by concurrent access to shared data in large databases. Flat transaction model is suitable for database applications characterized by short duration transactions and competitive access to shared data. The applications characterized by long duration with cooperative transactions require the need for extended/advanced transaction models.

Review Questions

1.   What is a transaction?
2.   What are the states of a transaction?
3.   Write about ACID property.
4.   What are the two types of transaction execution?
5.   How transactions are classified?
6.   Describe the criteria for defining the correctness of the database.
7.   What is meant by serializability?
8.   Write the limitations of serializability based correctness criteria.
9.   Explain the various non-serializable correctness criteria for database systems.
10. What is the use of a concurrency control algorithm?
11. What are the three basic techniques used to design concurrency control algorithms?

12. Explain locking concurrency control algorithm?

13. What is a transaction model?

14. Write about flat transaction model?

15. Discuss the various extended transaction models.

References

1. N.S. Barghouti and G.E. Kaiser, "Concurrency control in advanced database applications", ACM Computing Surveys, Vol. 23, No. 3, Pp. 269-317, 1991.

2. P.A. Bernstein and N. Eric, "Principles of transaction processing, second edition", Morgan Kaufmann Publishers, Elsevier, 2009.

3. B. Bhargava, "Concurrency control in database systems", IEEE Transactions on Knowledge and Data Engineering, Vol. 11, No. 1, Pp. 3-16, 1999.

4. P.K Chrysanthis and K. Ramamritham, "A taxonomy of correctness criteria in database applications", The VLDB Journal, Vol. 5, Pp. 85–97, 1996.

5. U. Dayal, M. Hsu and R. Ladin, "A Transaction Model for Long-Running Activities", In Proceedings of the 17th International Conference on Very Large Data Bases, Pp. 113-122, Spain, 1991.

6. A.K. Elmagarmid, "Transaction Models For Advanced Database Applications", CSD-TR-91-022, Computer Science Technical Reports, Department of Computer Science, Purdue University, 1991.

7. S. Meenakshi and V. Thiagarasu, "Correctness Criteria for Transaction Processing: A Survey and Analysis", International Journal of Applied Research & Studies, ISSN: 2278-9480, Vol. I, No. I, Mid-116, 2012.

8. S. Meenakshi and V. Thiagarasu, "Constructive Review of Transaction Models in Database Systems", International Journal of Advanced Research in Computer Science, ISSN: 0976-5697, Vol. 4, No. 4, Pp. 351-356, 2013.

9. A. Thomasian, "Concurrency Control: Methods, Performance and Analysis", ACM computing surveys, Vol. 20, No. 1, Pp. 71-119, 1998.

CHAPTER 5

LEARNING OF ACTIVE DATABASE SYSTEMS

Key Features

- Need for Active Mechanism in Database Systems
- Functions of Active Database Systems
- Active Rule Execution Model
- Active Information System
- Abstract Architecture of Active Database Systems
- Applications of Active Database Systems

5.1. Introduction

As the use of database systems are grown, users have demanded more functionality from database systems with the purpose of making it easier to develop advanced applications. Active database system is one of the advanced database system which provides active mechanism into database systems. Enriching database systems with active mechanism provide the ability to detect the occurrence of events and respond to them automatically in a timely manner without user or application intervention. Active database system is implemented through active rules which are in the form of event-condition-action (ECA) rules paradigm.

This chapter presents the need for active mechanism in database systems. The active database system provides number of features such as integrity constraint enforcement, derived data maintenance, triggers, alerters, protection and version control and gather statistics for query optimization. The process of augmenting the active mechanism into database systems requires the various capabilities such as rule specification, event detection, rule scheduling and execution.

This chapter describes the functions of active database system that includes the specification and the execution of the active rules. This chapter explains the execution model of active database system with its various phases. This chapter also presents the several issues for developing rule execution model of the active database system. This chapter specifies about active information system. This chapter discusses the abstract architecture and implementation of the active database system. The active database system is implemented into the existing database systems using layered or integrated architectural approaches. Most of the developmental efforts on the active database system have opted for integrated architecture. Finally this chapter presents the applications of active database systems in various domains.

5.2.   Need for Active Mechanism in Database Systems

In general, conventional database systems are viewed as a passive repository for managing data in response to the user requests or application program and not initiating any operations on their own. The relational DBMS based on relational model is successful for supporting business data processing applications that handle structured data. However applications that handles unstructured data such as images, voice, text document which are difficult to represent in the relational database system. In order to overcome the limitations of relational database systems, OODBSs and ORDBSs are introduced. Object-oriented and object-relational database systems provide features for modeling, storing and manipulating complex objects with object-oriented programming systems.

In order to satisfy the requirements of advanced applications, the field of database systems is aimed at increasing the functionality and performance of databases systems. In the recent past, one of the advanced database system namely active database system which provides active mechanism for monitoring the changes in database state and initiate appropriate actions automatically without user intervention, which is important for many advanced applications. In the active database system, the active behavior is incorporated using event-condition-action (ECA) rules paradigm. The active database system provides number of features such as integrity constraint enforcement, derived data maintenance, triggers, alerters, protection and version control and gather statistics for query optimization.

Enriching database systems with active mechanism provide the ability to perform certain operations automatically, when specified events occur and particular conditions being satisfied based on the knowledge stored in the form of ECA rules within DBMS. The implementation of the active database system moves the active behavior from the application into the DBMS. Rather than the application code have to explicitly query the database at predefined intervals in order to find out if particular events are occurred, ECA rules provide timely response to events based on the active functionality defined within the DBMS. Moving the active mechanism into the DBMS enable the application developers to easily find and modify the rules, when application requirements change. Also it is possible to maintain the rules up-to-date without modifying the rest of the application code. Active database system is important for many real time applications such as medical, financial, decision support systems and network management which depend on data monitoring activities.

5.3.   Functions of Active Database Systems

A database system coupled with ECA rules is known as the active database system (ADBS) which provides active mechanism to monitor changes in the database state and initiate appropriate actions automatically without user intervention based on the ECA rules stored in the DBMS. The ADBS is important for applications that require automatic reaction in response to the occurrence of certain events that are taking place either inside or outside of the database systems.

In order to achieve the active mechanism, the active database system performs the following two functions: (a) specifying the reactive behavior–rule languages are used to define the syntax and specification of ECA rules, (b) executing the reactive behavior–mechanisms for monitoring relevant situations and reacting to them and this function is carried out by the ADBS through a strategy called rule processing.

5.3.1.   *Specification of Reactive Behavior*

The active database system is centered on the notion of rule. The reactive behavior of a system is specified by means of rules which describe the situations to be monitored and the reactions of the system when these situations are encountered.

Thus rules are syntactic constructs by means of which the reactions of the system are specified.

<table>
<tr><td>Define rule rule-name</td></tr>
<tr><td>On <event></td></tr>
<tr><td>If <condition></td></tr>
<tr><td>Then <action></td></tr>
</table>

Figure 5.1: General Syntax of ECA Rule Definition

Active rules are defined based on the ECA rule paradigm. A rule definition language provides constructs for specifying rules. The result of the rule specification activity is a set of rule definitions or rules. Depending on the rule language the elements of a rule is defined and the general syntax for defining an ECA-rule is shown in Figure 5.1.

The define rule clause of a rule defines a unique rule-name of the rule. The on-clause of a rule defines the types of events that may trigger the rule. The if-clause of a rule defines the conditions that are evaluated when the rules are triggered. The action after then-clause of a rule is a sequence of operations to be performed when the rule is triggered and its condition is satisfied.

However in certain active database systems the rule format has specified in different formats: EC-A (Condition-Action, where only the condition and action are specified. If the event is omitted then the rule is executed when the condition becomes true) and E-CA (Event-Action, where only event and action are specified. If the condition is omitted it is always true).

Event Specification

An event is a relevant happening that are to be monitored by the ADBS. The event part of a rule specifies the situations to which the rule may be able to respond. Rules are triggered on the occurrence of various events such as database operations, occurrence of database states and transitions between states. An event is categorized as either primitive or composite.

Primitive events are atomic events which are associated with a point in time. Primitive events are defined in the system. Primitive events are classified based on their origin as internal and external. Internal events are associated with the access to the database and the external events are produced by the occurrences outside the database in its environment.

The various primitive internal events are:

- Database operation events occur at the beginning or at the end of a database operation. Thus the event definition has to specify if the instances have to occur before or after the operation has performed. In relational database systems these events are SQL modification operations such as insert, update, delete and the retrieval operation select applied on a certain table. In object oriented database systems data operations are performed through the methods invocation that access persistent collection of objects. Method events are signaled when the persistent objects are created (constructor is called) or deleted (destructor is called) or when methods modifying or retrieving objects are invoked.

- Transaction events occur before or after a transaction operation such as begin, end, abort and commit.

The various primitive external events are:

- Temporal (absolute/relative) events occur either at absolute time points (e.g., 6.8.2013, 10.00 A.M) or periodically (e.g., every day at 10.00 A.M).

- Abstract events are user-defined events whose occurrences are directly signaled and they are explicitly raised by the user and associated with a point in time.

Composite events express more semantics than primitive events. Composite events are defined as a combination of primitive and possibly by other composite events. The meaningful ways to build composite events from its constituent events are usually specified through event algebra that defines certain event constructors. Thus composite events consist of primitive or composite events combined with logical operators. The various composite event constructors are:

- Disjunction – Events are combined using the "or" operator. The disjunction of two events, event1 and event2, is raised when either of event1 or event2 occurs.
- Conjunction – Events are combined using the "and" operator. The conjunction of two events, event1 and event2, is raised when both event1 and event2 occurs.
- Sequence – Events are to be raised one after another and in the right order. The sequence of two events, event1 and event2, is raised when event1 and event2 occur in that order.
- Closure – The closure of an event, event1 is raised exactly once regardless of the number of times event1 occurs.
- Negation – The negation of an event, event1 is raised if event1 does not occur in a given time interval.
- History – The history of an event, event1 is raised, if event1 occurs a given number of times.

For the last three event constructors, it is appropriate to define time intervals in which composition of events should take place. The definition of a time interval is mandatory for negation and optional for history and closure. Triggering events can also be parameterized. When a parameterized event occurs, values related to the event are bound to the event parameters and these parameter values are referred in rule conditions or actions.

Condition Specification

The condition of a rule checks the state of a database at the time when the rule event occurs. The condition part of a rule is usually expressed as a Boolean expression, a predicate, or a set of queries and it is satisfied if the expression evaluates to true or all the queries return non-empty results. In addition to the current state of the database, the condition may access the state of the database at the time of event occurrence by use of event parameters.

Action Specification

The action part of a rule specifies the operations to be performed when the rule is triggered and its condition is satisfied. In general an action can be database operations, transaction commands or arbitrary executable routines. Therefore during the execution of an action certain events may also occur. This may lead to the triggering of other rules which is called nested or cascaded rule triggering. The action may access besides the current database state, the database state at the time of event occurrence and the time of condition evaluation which are performed by parameter passing.

5.3.2. *Rule Processing*

The behavior of active database system depends on, not only the set of rules given to the system but also the strategy of rule processing adopted by the system. Applications programs are executed until an event is signaled. If an event is signaled, the control moves to the rule processing. Signaled events trigger appropriate rules which are inserted into the set of triggered rules. Then, rules are selected according to certain criteria from this set, their condition is evaluated and finally their action is executed. If the execution of the action signals further events, further rules are inserted into the set of triggered rules. When the set of triggered rules is empty, the control move backs to the application program.

Rule Processing Activities

The various activities that are performed by the ADBS during rule processing are described as the following.

- **Event signaling** - The primitive event detector detects primitive events when it occurs. Also the composite event detector considers the primitive event occurrences that contribute to the composite events. The detection is carried out until the composite event detector arrives to a final state and no more composite events may be detected. The result of event detection is the signaling of events. First primitive events are signaled and then composite events are signaled. Then the system assigns unique timestamp for events.

- **Rule triggering** - This phase is performed immediately after event signaling. It applies to only rule events. Considering the events in the order given by their timestamps, corresponding rule definitions are retrieved from the set. For each retrieved definition, a rule instance is created. Rule instances are inserted into conflict set, which is the set of all triggered and not yet executed rules. In order to execute the triggered rules a selection criterion is to be applied.

- **Rule selection** - When multiple rules are triggered by a single event or by many different events at the same time, the active database system provides certain techniques to schedule the execution order of multiple triggered rules at a given point in time. In the ADBS, rule scheduler uses the deterministic (static) and non-deterministic (dynamic) priority policies to specify the order in which rules are selected for execution. The three techniques that are used by the rule scheduler during rule processing are: (a) one rule is selected arbitrarily for execution in the set; (b) sequential execution of all rules in a set; c) parallel execution of all rules in a set. Parallel execution of rules is achieved through concurrent execution of all rules by using a nested transaction model.

- **Rule evaluation and execution** - Rule evaluation evaluates the condition of the selected rule. If the condition is satisfied the action is executed. Rule execution is also called as rule firing which represents the phase where the action of the selected rule is executed.

In order to achieve the active functionality for monitoring and reacting to specific event occurrence in database systems each ADBS has a knowledge model that is used to define the specification of ECA rules and also an execution model that determines the processing of rules at runtime.

5.4. Active Rule Execution Model

Active database systems provide an ideal platform for supporting today's complex applications in order to express an event-driven and constraint-driven system environment. In active database systems, an application defines rules and specifies the desired behavior of each rule in the form of ECA. Once a set of rules is defined, the active database system monitors the relevant events. For each rule if an event occurs then the system evaluates the rule's condition and if the rule's condition is true then the rule's action part is executed.

In order to monitor and react to specific event occurrences in the application, each active database system possesses a knowledge and execution model. Rule definition language that is used to define the syntax and specification of ECA rules for describing reactive behavior generally referred to as the knowledge model. The knowledge model describes the structural characteristics of rules such as types of events, context of conditions and actions. An execution model determines the processing of rules at runtime and it captures the runtime characteristics of rule processing include event detection, signaling of events, scheduling of rules and rule execution.

Phases of Rule Execution Model

The execution model goes beyond the knowledge model and describes how the rules are evaluated at runtime and hence rule execution semantics is an important aspect in ADBS. The use of active rules in advanced applications creates new challenges for the development of rule execution model to provide the effective rule processing mechanism at runtime in active database systems.

The various phases performed during rule execution are shown in Figure 5.2 and are described as the following:

- Event signaling – The signaling phase detects and signals the occurrence of the event.
- Rule triggering – The event activates the corresponding active rules in the triggering phase.
- Condition evaluation – The condition part of the triggered rules are evaluated in the evaluation phase. The rule conflict problem occurs when the conditions of more than one trigger rules are evaluated to be true.
- Rule scheduling – The scheduling phase indicates the order to process the rule conflict set when multiple rules are triggered at the same time.
- Execution phase – The execution phase processes the scheduled triggered rules.

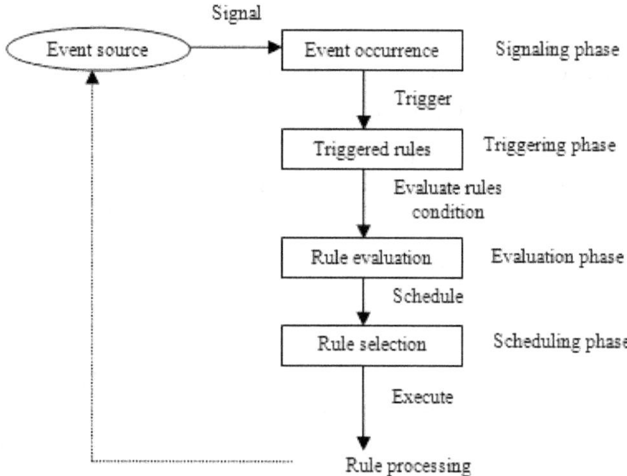

Figure 5.2: Phases of Rule Execution Model

In active database systems, the semantics of rule execution is integrated with the transaction execution framework. When an event occurring in a transaction triggers a rule, then the transaction is called the triggering (parent) transaction and the transaction which executes the triggered rule is called the triggered (sub) transaction.

Issues of Developing Rule Execution Model

The rule processing behavior is complex and the several issues concerned with the development of rule execution model of active database system are the following.

- **Rule processing point (Coupling modes):** The rule processing point that specifies the time when a triggered transaction is executed with respect to the triggering transaction or event. That is coupling modes specifies when the rule's condition is evaluated with respect to the triggering event (E-C coupling) and when the rule's action is executed with respect to the condition evaluation (C-A coupling). The three basic coupling modes used with E-C coupling and C-A coupling are immediate, deferred and detached or decoupled.
  - Immediate – In the immediate coupling mode, the triggered transaction is executed immediately after the event is signaled.
  - Deferred – In the deferred coupling mode, the triggered transaction is executed at the end of the triggering transaction, but before the commit of the triggering transaction.
  - Detached or decoupled – In the case of detached coupling mode, the triggered transaction is executed as a separate transaction.

In the case of immediate and deferred modes, the triggered transactions are essentially the subtransactions of the triggering transaction. But in the case of detached mode, the triggered transaction is started directly after event signaling and it is independent of the triggering transaction. In the detached coupling mode, the triggered transaction is executed concurrently with the triggering transaction. A detached transaction can commit or abort regardless the termination of the triggering transaction. Thus the commit and abort dependencies as present in the immediate and deferred coupling modes are not exists in the detached mode. The immediate and detached mode can cause long delays in a transaction. Detached mode increases concurrency and well result in long delays. Several other coupling modes such as causally dependent and independent modes and sequential causally and exclusive causally dependent modes are proposed for flexible rule execution.

- **Rule processing granularity:** Rule processing granularity refers to the aspect of determining how often the system runs the rule evaluation procedure and is defined at different levels. The finest granularity is 'always' which means that rules are processed as soon as any rule's triggering event occurs. At the next level of granularity the system checks for triggering rules at the time of occurrence of database operations. Finally coarse granularity is at transaction level and the rules are evaluated at the end of each transaction after the execution of data manipulation statements.

Another issue related with rule granularity is either instance-oriented or set-oriented rule execution. With an instance-oriented execution, a rule is triggered once for each database instance triggering the rule and satisfying the rule condition. In set-oriented execution, a rule is executed once for all database instances triggering the rule and satisfying the rule condition. Hence an execution model is instance-oriented means, it instantiates rule for each event occurrence of the rule and set-oriented means it instantiates rule for a set of event occurrences.

- **Rule scheduling:** When multiple rules are triggered at the same time, scheduling mechanism determines their execution priority and the execution semantics: sequential or concurrent.

- **Termination:** The action execution of a rule may cause the occurrence of some new events. These new events may in turn, trigger other rules. This could lead to an infinite loop by a chain of triggering. The termination of rule processing is often unpredictable. The use of termination analysis tools are helpful in highlighting the potential cycles in an active rule set.

- **Confluence:** This property specifies whether the execution order of non-prioritized rules can make any difference in the final database state.

In active database systems, the semantics of rule execution is integrated with the transaction execution framework. Rules are triggered in the context of transaction execution and to maintain the correctness of the operation, most of the ADBS rule execution model uses transaction management mechanism of the underlying DBMS. Thus the execution of rules has the same semantics as the execution of transactions in database systems.

When several rules are executed in concurrent, a flexible advanced transaction model is required to perform concurrent rule execution in an effective manner. The concurrent rule execution brings a concurrency control issue that needs to be addressed.

Rules are processed according to an execution model and thus the mechanism to execute triggered rules must be effective and constructed in such a way that predictability can be ensured in real-time systems. This puts the demand on rule execution model to obtain good performance on rule triggering, condition evaluation and action execution.

5.5.   Active Information System

Design of an active database system is viewed in two ways. One is the active database system is a database system with active rules. The other view is the active database system is a specialized information system. Information system is used to provide a service, which is semantic entities entailing consideration that span the lifecycle of the application system. Services are initially defined and modeled as sequences of tasks resulting in various flow based representations. Services are interactive in nature involving user sessions with one or more users. An interactive service need not be a closed atomic operation and is also not isolated from one another. It may involve many intermediate states where the external environment may influence the flow of the computation. Two or more interactive services may be intertwined in such a way that their operations cannot be serialized.

The distinction between a database and an information system is best appreciated based on their functions. The task of a passive database is to store data and answer queries. The task of an information system is to provide services. The general model of an information system is in the form of a collection of semantic services. Today most of the database systems provide features that go beyond the management of static data and most information systems are powered by a database.

The active database system provides active capabilities in the form of ECA rules to detect the occurrence of events and perform trigger actions as a result of the detection, according to the condition. By contrast, the active information system maintains its dynamic integrity and also supports ongoing interaction with environment rather than transform a given problem to a solution. However, there is a growing realization that services are best designed using models of interaction, developed largely in reactive system domain.

Active information system (AIS) is an interactive service-providing system rather than mere data transformation engines. The AIS deals with passive functions in traditional database systems and active functions in application environment together for active data processing. Active information system describes the function specifications in the application environment more availably and makes the reaction actively for the different events in the application environment. An active information system must provide a knowledge model and execution model for supporting reactive behavior. The knowledge model supports the description of active functionality in the form of ECA rules. The mechanism of ECA rule processing includes rule specification, rule management and rule execution. Developing an active information system for active data processing in application environment causes lot of issues while executing active rules.

5.6. Abstract Architecture of Active Database Systems

The behavior of active rules depends on the rule processing strategy adopted by the execution model of an active database system. In order to implement the functionalities of the rule execution model as shown in Figure 5.2, an abstract architecture of the active database system consists of several principal components (rectangles in the figure) and data stores (circles in the figure) is presented in Figure 5.3.

Once set of active rules are defined, the ADBS performs the principal processes as follows:

- The Event Detector detects the events of interest to the system. Data modification events are noticed from the database.
- The Condition Monitor evaluates the conditions of rules associated with the detected events and stores the rules whose conditions are evaluated to true in a conflict set.
- The Scheduler chooses and executes a rule from the conflict set according to the conflict resolution policy.
- The Query Evaluator executes the database queries, such as transaction queries and conditions and actions resulting from the rules. When evaluating such queries, the query evaluator accesses not only the current state of the database, if necessary, past states and history of the database.

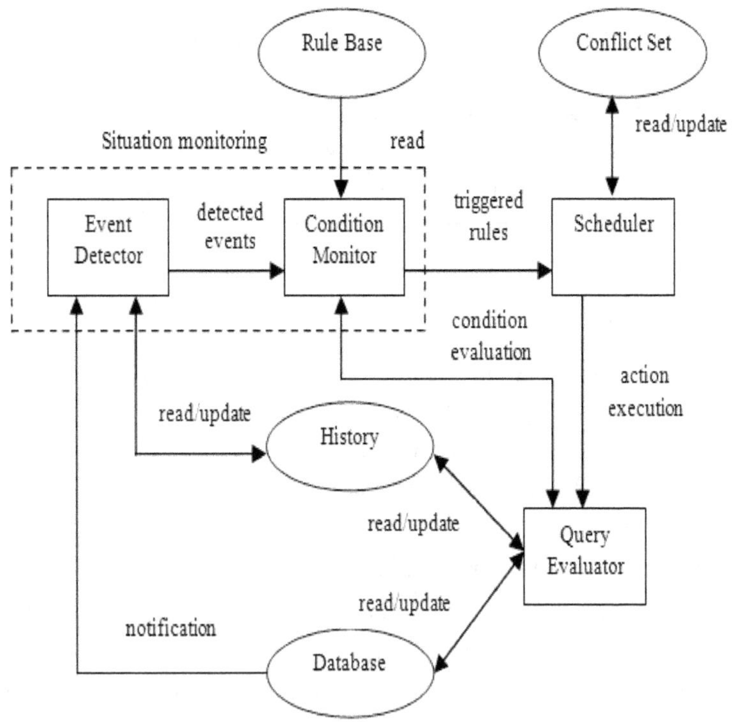

Figure 5.3: Abstract Architecture of ADBS

5.6.1. *Layered and Integrated Architecture*

The functionality of each of the components as shown in Figure 5.3 depends on the knowledge and execution models of the active database system to be supported, which in turn are influenced by the environment within which the active database system is being developed. The development of the active database system is carried out in two ways. One approach is to develop the entire database system from scratch. However this approach leads to a costlier one in terms of hardware and software. The other approach is, to embed the ADBS into the existing database systems. The two categories of architecture identified for implementing the active database system into the existing database systems are layered and integrated architectures which are described as the following.

Layered Architecture

In a layered architecture, the active functionality is implemented on top of an existing database system with no modification to the underlying DBMS. Layered architecture requires that a layer be built, through which all ECA rule specifications are routed. All operations using active functionality must communicate through the layer and it is responsible for monitoring situations and executing appropriate rules based on the rule processing technique provided by the transaction manager of the underlying DBMS. The advantage of this architecture is that no modification is required to the source code of the conventional database system. However the disadvantage of this approach is the lack of direct communication with the underlying DBMS components such as transaction manager, lock manager which limit the performance and functionality of the active behavior.

Integrated Architecture

In an integrated architecture, the active functionality is embedded in the existing conventional database system as shown in Figure 5.4. In this architecture the kernel or core functionality of the underlying DBMS is enhanced to include situation monitoring, event detection and extended transaction management to support rule processing. Hence the modification to the source code of the conventional database system is to be required.

The various advantages of this architecture include: DBMS is responsible for optimizing ECA rules, DBMS functionality is extended, modularity and maintenance of applications is better and easier, and do not require any changes to existing application. This architecture is flexible and is used to directly accessing the core functionality of the underlying DBMS and also frees the designer of the active database system from the limitations of the layered approach.

Most of the developmental efforts on the active database system have opted for integrated architecture.

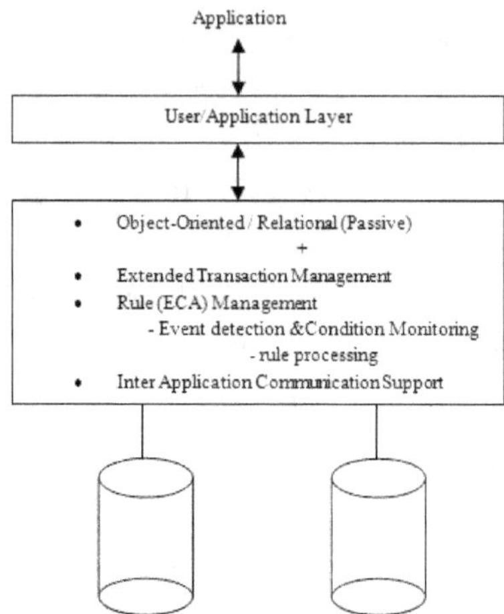

Figure 5.4: Integrated Active Database Architecture

5.6.2. *Implementation of Active Database Systems*

In general the active database system is implemented as extensions to a DBMS based on the client/server architecture principle. When building an active database, a decision is to be made about the type of architecture used for integrating active functionality into the database systems. In general any ADBS must have an underlying DBMS, a facility to define a set of rules, an event detector, a condition evaluator and an action processor and the organization of these components varies over different database systems. An active database system is built upon DBMS using layered or integrated architectural approaches. Research and development efforts on active database systems and commercial implementations have focused on integrating active capabilities in the context of relational, object-oriented and object-relational database systems.

Early researches on the active database system are focused on integrating active capabilities in the context of relational database systems. In active relational database systems, active rules or triggers monitor changes performed to given tables. Triggers are executed immediately before or after the transactional statement that performs the table change; the condition is typically an SQL predicate, and the action is either a collection of SQL statements or a stored procedure or a program written in a database programming language. Thus active relational database systems are limited to simple database events like database modifications such as insert delete and modify operations, events related to transactions such as commit and abort. A number of research prototypes are developed to integrate active behavior into the relational database systems which include Starburst, Ariel and POSTGRES.

Object-oriented database systems provide richer event type system such as method invocation, temporal events, user defined events and composition of events through event algebra. The concept of rule inheritance and overriding provides the facility for reusing and redefining the rules. The integration of the active database system with object-oriented database systems provides many benefits than relational database systems. Several research prototypes are proposed to incorporate active rules into object-oriented systems which include HiPAC, Adam, Ode, ACOOD, NAOS, SAMOS, Sentinel, Chimera, REACH, EXACT and TriGS.

Object-relational database system supports object-relational model by combining the benefits of both relational and object-oriented data model. Object-relational database systems support relational technologies (SQL, ODBC, transaction management and concurrency control), user-defined data types, and handling of complex data with object-oriented concepts. The integration of the active database system with the object-relational database system effectively supports advanced applications than conventional relational and object-oriented database systems. The object-relational database standard SQL3 and the various commercial object-relational database products such as Oracle, Ingres, Informix and Sybase provide active features in the form of triggers.

5.7. Applications of Active Database Systems

Active database system provides an elegant mechanism for capturing many real life applications which automatically perform certain operations in response to certain events occurring with certain conditions being satisfied. The active database system supports applications with the facility of specifying rules that monitor changes in the database that inform applications of interesting changes. Applications of active database systems are range from handling integrity constraints to performing complex database changes.

Categories of ADBS Applications

Active database systems are used for the following various categories of applications:

- Closed database applications – This type of application involves the use of active functionality within the database and without reference to the external devices or systems. Examples of such applications are automatic statistical analysis (e.g. making market predictions), maintaining high level data consistency (e.g. propagating load requirements between connected elements in an architectural design), and altering users to special conditions (e.g. warning production managers of low inventory levels).

- Open database applications – In this category, a database is used in conjunction with monitoring devices to record and respond to situations outside the database. Open database applications require a more proactive approach in which system actually controls actions to be taken in the real world. Examples of such application include air traffic flow management, communications network control, medical monitoring, and battlefield threat assessment.

- Database system extensions – Active rules are used as a primitive mechanism for supporting extensions to core database functionality. It includes integrity constraints, materialized views, derived data, data modeling constructs, triggers and automatic screen updating in the context of database change.

The active database system is also applied for various application domains such as cooperative applications, e-business applications, web applications, business processes system, ubiquitous web services, continuous query system, biometric system and healthcare system.

5.8. Summary

This chapter has discussed the concept and the need for active mechanism in database systems. This chapter has explained the functions of active database systems that included the specification of ECA rule syntax and the rule processing activities. This chapter has also described the knowledge and execution model of the active database system. This chapter also explained the various phases and the issues for developing rule execution model of the active database system. This chapter has specified about active information system. This chapter has provided the abstract architecture of the active database system and also presented the implementation of the active database system. Finally this chapter has presented the applications of active database systems in various domains.

Review Questions

1. What is active database system?
2. Describe the need for an active database system?
3. Write the features of active database system?
4. What are the two functions of active database system?
5. Write the general syntax for defining an ECA-rule in active database system.
6. Describe how the reactive behavior of a system is specified in active database system.

7. Describe the various activities of rule processing in active database system.

8. What is the need of knowledge model in active database system?

9. What is the role of execution model in active database system?

10. Explain the various phases of rule execution model in active database system.

11. What is meant by coupling modes?

12. Write the three types of coupling modes.

13. Explain the various issues concerned with the development of rule execution model in active database system.

14. Write a note on active information system.

15. Explain the two architectural categories used to implement active database system.

16. Explain the applications of active database systems.

References

1. F. Bry, M. Eckert, P.L. Patranjan and I. Romanenko, "Realizing Business Processes with ECA rules: Benefits, Challenges, Limits", In Proceedings of the International Workshop on Principles and Practice of Semantic Web, Pp. 48-62, 2006.

2. A.P. Buchmann, "Architecture of Active Database Systems", In N.Paton (ed.) Active Rules in Database Systems, Chapter 2, Pp. 29-48, Springer, 1999.

3. S. Chakravarthy, "Architectures and monitoring techniques for active databases: An evaluation", Data & Knowledge Engineering, Elsevier, Vol. 16, No. 1, Pp. 1-26, July 1995.

4. M. Cilia, "Active Database Management Systems", Idea Group Inc., 2006.

5. M. Cilia and A. Buchmann, "An active functionality service for e-business applications", ACM SIGMOD Record, Vol. 31, No. 1, Pp. 24-30, 2002.

6. U. Dayal, E.N. Hanson and J. Widom, "Active Database Systems", In W. Kim, editor, Modern Database Systems: The Object Model, Interoperability, and Beyond, Pp. 434-456, ACM Press, 1994.

7. R.S. Devarkonda, "Object-relational Database Systems - the road ahead", ACM Crossroads, Vol. 7, No. 3, Pp. 15-18, March 2001.

8. A.K. Dittrich and E. Simon, "Active Database Systems: Expectations, Commercial Experience, and Beyond", Active Rules in Database Systems, Monographs in Computer Science, Pp. 367-404, Springer, 1999.

9. K.R. Dittrich, S. Gatziu and A. Geppert, "The active database management system manifesto: A rulebase of ADBMS features", In Proceedings of the 2nd International Workshop on Rules in Databases, Lecture Notes in Computer Science, Vol. 985, Pp. 1-17, Springer, 1995.

10. K. Dube and B. Wu, "A generic approach to computer-based Clinical Practice Guideline management using the ECA Rule paradigm and active databases", International Journal of Technology Management (IJTM), Vol. 47, No. 1/2/3, Pp. 75-95, 2009.

11. D. Goldin, S. Srinivasa and V. Srikanti, "Active Databases as Information Systems", In Proceedings of the International Database Engineering and Applications Symposium, Pp. 123-130, 2004.

12. J.Y. Jung, J. Park, S.K. Han and K. Lee, "An ECA-based framework for decentralized coordination of ubiquitous web services", Information and Software Technology, Elsevier, Vol. 49, No. 11-12, Pp. 1141-1161, 2007.

13. N.W. Paton and O. Diaz, "Active database systems", ACM Computing Surveys, Vol. 31, No. 1, Pp. 63-103, 1999.

14. K. Rabuzin, M. Malekovic and M. Baca, "A Multimodal Biometric System Based upon the Active Database Paradigm", Journal of Management, Informatics and Human Resources, Vol. 39, No. 7, Slovenia, Pp. 425-431, 2006.

15. E. Simon and A.K. Dittrich, "Promises and Realities of Active Database Systems", In Proceedings of the 21st VLDB Conference, Pp. 642-653, Zurich, Switzerland, 1995.

CHAPTER 6

ACTIVE OBJECT-RELATIONAL DATABASE SYSTEMS

Key Features

- Triggers in SQL3 Standard
- Classification and Use of Trigger Systems
- Oracle Triggers
- Design and Implementation Issues of AORDBS

6.1. Introduction

The development efforts on active database systems are focused to extend the functionality of conventional database systems with powerful rule processing capabilities. Active database system is implemented in DBMS using layered or integrated architectural approaches. Active mechanism is important for many advanced data management applications such as e-commerce, business processes system, ubiquitous web services, biometric system and healthcare monitoring system. The active database system is implemented in commercial database systems in a limited form of triggers.

Object-relational database systems have gained acceptance as a powerful technology for handling complex database applications by extending the relational database system with object-oriented features such as user defined data types, reference attributes, inheritance and polymorphism. An object-relational database system allows the users to effectively model and manipulate the unstructured data and also to use object-oriented concepts for application development without losing the benefits of SQL with all the necessary features of a commercial-strength DBMS.

Integration of an active database system with an object-relational database system is referred to as active object-relational database system (AORDBS) that extends the normal functionality of the object-relational database system with support to monitor the changes to the database state and react to specific situations automatically without user intervention. The SQL3 standard and the various commercial object-relational database systems such as Oracle, MSSQL, Sybase, and Ingres provide active mechanism in the form of triggers. Triggers allow users to specify constraints that govern how data are modified and it execute actions automatically when certain conditions are detected in the database. In SQL3, triggers are expressed by means of event-condition-action (ECA) rules.

This chapter explains the knowledge and execution model of SQL3 standard for trigger definition and processing. In addition, this chapter specifies the features of triggers in SQL3 standard and also in commercial database systems. This chapter describes the classification and the use of triggers in database systems. This chapter also illustrates the use of triggers in object-relational database system using Oracle triggers. Finally this chapter discusses the various issues related to the design and implementation of generic active rule system in active object-relational database system.

6.2.   Triggers in SQL3 Standard

Triggers extend the database systems with the capability to respond automatically to certain specific events that are taking place in database systems. Triggers are the important component of commercial object-relational database systems since active rules are required for advanced applications to perform (react) certain operations automatically when specified events occur and particular conditions are met. The utility and functionality of triggers are established in various commercial object-relational database products such as Oracle, Ingres, Informix, Sybase, DB2, and MSSQL. The SQL3 standard is characterized as object-oriented SQL which standardizes the functions of triggers. An SQL trigger is a facility (procedural technique) that allows database designers to instruct the database system to perform certain operations every time automatically, whenever an application performs specified operations on particular tables.

A trigger in SQL3 standard is an ECA rule that is activated by a database state transition and SQL3 predicate is a condition and SQL3 statements is an action. A trigger is activated whenever a specified event occurs and the event is usually an INSERT, DELETE, or UPDATE operations on a particular table monitored by the trigger. Once the trigger is activated, an optional specified condition is checked and if the condition is true, an action is executed. If the condition is omitted, it is considered as true and an action is executed.

The SQL3 standard captures active behavior by using two kinds of constructs such as knowledge model and execution model.

6.2.1.   Knowledge Model

The knowledge model describes the structural characteristics of rules such as types of events, context of conditions and actions. In SQL3, triggers are identified by unique name which are expressed by means of ECA rules using the syntax as shown in Figure 6.1.

A trigger is activated whenever a specified event occurs, and the event specifies the database operations usually an insert, delete or update operation on a particular table monitored by the trigger. The condition is expressed as an arbitrary SQL predicate involving complex queries. The action can be any sequence of database operations that include SQL manipulation statement, user defined functions and procedures. Triggers have an activation time such as before, after or instead of the triggering event, and a granularity either row-level or statement-level.

In the SQL3 standard, the keywords BEFORE and AFTER specifies the trigger activation time i.e. specify whether the trigger action is to be executed BEFORE or AFTER the triggering statement. The REFERENCING clause allows the trigger to access the old and new values of the row or statement affected by the triggering event, by means of transition variables (OLD and NEW) and transition tables (OLD TABLE and NEW TABLE).

```
<Trigger definition > :: =  CREATE TRIGGER <trigger-name>
                  {BEFORE|AFTER}<trigger-event> ON <table-name>
                  [REFERENCING {OLD [AS] <old-value-tuple-name>
                  |NEW [AS] <new-value-tuple-name>
                  |OLD_TABLE [AS] <old-value-table-name>
                  |NEW_TABLE [AS] <new-value-table-name>}]
<Triggered event> :: =    INSERT| DELETE|UPDATE [OF <column-names>
  <Triggered action>  :: =  [FOR EACH {ROW |STATEMENT}]
                  [WHEN <condition>] <triggered SQL statement>
```

Figure 6.1: Syntax of SQL3 Trigger

SQL3 provides the notion of granularity to define how many times the trigger is executed for the particular event. The FOR EACH ROW refers to a row-level trigger, which is executed on each tuple modification of the triggering event. The FOR EACH STATEMENT refers to a statement-level trigger, which is executed once for an event regardless of the number of tuples affected.

A WHEN clause specifies an additional condition to be checked once the trigger rule is fired and before the action is executed. If the WHEN clause is missing, the condition is supposed to be true and the trigger action is executed as soon as the trigger event occurs. The action is executed when the rule is triggered and its condition is true. SQL3 allows multiple action statements in triggers, each of which is executed according to the order they are written.

6.2.2. Execution Model

The execution model captures the runtime characteristics of rule processing includes event detection, signaling of events, scheduling of rules and rule execution. The various dimensions of the execution model of SQL3 are shown in Table 6.1.

A trigger is fired whenever a table is modified by the triggering events such as insert, update, delete. Once a trigger is fired, it executes SQL statements defined in the trigger action. Each trigger has access to the old value and new values of the changed data by means of transition variables, such as OLD ROW and NEW ROW. The reactive behavior is handled in a timely manner using a BEFORE or an AFTER trigger. A BEFORE trigger is activated before the operation modifies the table executed, while an AFTER trigger is activated after the modifying operation executes. The granularity of a trigger is specified as either FOR EACH ROW or FOR EACH STATEMENT, which refers to row-level and statement-level triggers respectively.

Table 6.1: Dimensions of the Execution Model of SQL3

DIMENSIONS	SQL3
EVENT-CONDITION Coupling	Immediate
CONDITION-ACTION Coupling	Immediate
Consumption Mode	None
Net-effect Policy	No
Priority	Creation time
Scheduling	Sequential
Error handling	Backtrack

The execution model of SQL3 should satisfy at least two requirements:

- Trigger actions must always be executed in consistent database states.
- All BEFORE triggers must be entirely executed before the database operations associated with the events mentioned in their event parts are executed and all AFTER trigger must be entirely executed after the execution of the database operations associated with their event parts.

The first requirement is satisfied by checking constraints every time the database is updated. The second requirement is met by executing any BEFORE trigger prior to any update to the database, and by executing any AFTER trigger after all updates caused by triggers of higher priority and by the operation associated with the event mentioned in the event part of the AFTER trigger have executed.

The behavior of triggers is based on the execution model and the existence of triggers in a database system affects its execution model significantly. The execution model determines the interaction of triggers and database applications. The development of an execution model is based on two dimensions such as the application and trigger granularities. The application granularity is the level at which trigger activation is detected. After each database command, the system checks whether there are activated triggers and executes them. The Figure 6.2 shows the options for choosing the application granularity which include database session, database transaction and database operation. The finer application granularity leads to more possibilities for trigger usage systems such as user notification, application procedures, communication, integrity enforcement and protection. If the application granularity is the database session, then messages can only be sent after the session has finished, which limits interaction with the user.

However, if the application granularity is a database command, then messages are sent after each command and it is possible to define triggers which interact with the user application. Therefore, the database command level granularity is better than other application granularities for trigger execution.

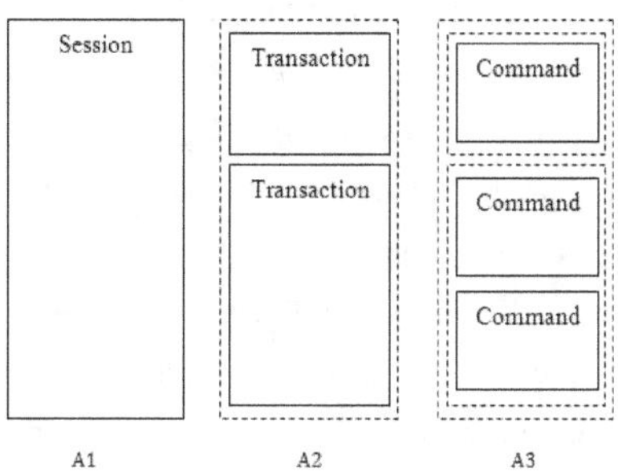

Figure 6.2: Application Granularities

The trigger granularity is the level of atomicity at which trigger components are executed and Figure 6.3 shows the various levels of trigger granularities.

In T2, event, condition and action are individually atomic and in T3, the low-level operations that constitute the event, condition and action are atomic and the granularity becomes finer from left to right.

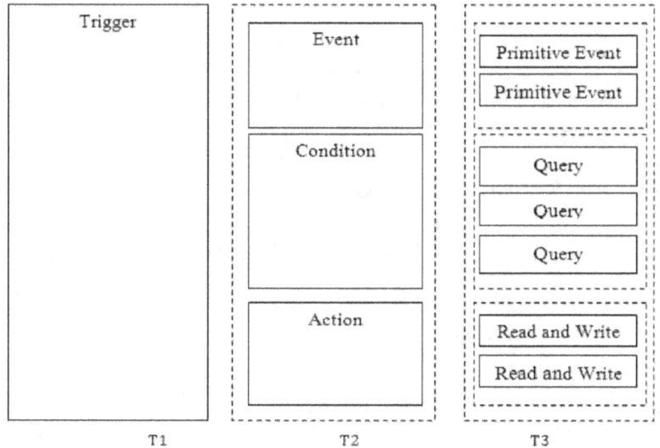

Figure 6.3: Trigger Granularities

For example, consider a trigger system based on application granularity A2, i.e. a database transaction Tr_i, and trigger granularity T2, i.e., a trigger split into its three basic components E_i, C_i, and A_i. Then an application run AG = $\{Tr_1, Tr_2, Tr_3,...Tr_n\}$ and trigger execution TG = $\{E_1, C_1, A_1, E_2, C_2, A_2,...E_m, C_m, A_m\}$. The outcome of the system is determined by the scheduler over AG and TG and the example schedule is < Tr_1, E_1, C_1, A_1, Tr2, E2, C_2, A_2...>. Clearly, only meaningful schedule should be generated and the semantics of such schedules should be defined by extending the transaction semantics.

In summary, in SQL3 standard each trigger reacts to a single event. The various considered events are inserting, delete, or update to a particular relation. For update events the attribute or set of attributes target of the modification can also be specified. The condition WHEN clause specifies an additional condition to be checked once the rule is triggered and before the action is executed. Conditions are predicates over the database state. In SQL the condition is expressed as an arbitrary SQL predicate potentially involving complex queries. The action is executed when the rule is triggered and its condition is true. The action may then prevent the event from taking place or it could undo the event (e.g. delete the inserted tuple). The action can be any sequence of database operations, even operations not connected in any way to the triggering event. In particular, the action can include any SQL data manipulation statement as well as invocations of user defined functions and procedures.

SQL3 Trigger Example

The Figure 6.4 shows an example of SQL3 trigger named as 'log-salary' which is used to log the changes of salaries in an employee table, when the specified condition is satisfied. The trigger rule imposes a condition that, when the salary of the employee increases by more than 10 percent, log-salary inserts the employee id, the old salary and new salary of employee into the table 'log-table-salary'.

```
CREATE TRIGGER log-salary
AFTER UPDATE OF salary ON employee
REFERENCING OLD ROW as oldrow
            NEW ROW as newrow
FOR EACH ROW
WHEN (newrow.salary > (oldrow.salary * 1.10))
INSERT INTO log-table-salary
    VALUES (oldrow.id, oldrow.salary, newrow.salary)
```

Figure 6.4: SQL3 Trigger

6.2.3. *Features of Triggers in SQL3 and Commercial Database Systems*

The various features provided by the SQL3 triggers are the following.

- An SQL3 trigger monitors to a single event, thus it is implicitly associated with table to which the monitored event refers.

- The trigger is executed before, after the triggering operation. Specification of trigger execution with once for each modified tuple (row-level trigger) or once for all the tuples that are changed in a database operation (statement-level trigger). The trigger condition and action can refer to both old and new values of tuples that are inserted, deleted or updated by the operation that triggered the rule.

- If an entire table is updated with an SQL update statement, a statement level trigger would execute only once, while a row level trigger would execute once for each tuple. In a row-level trigger the condition is evaluated on each tuple affected by triggering operation and if it holds the trigger action is executed on the tuple. By contrast, in a statement-level trigger, the trigger condition is evaluated once on all the tuples affected by the triggering operation and if it holds the trigger action is executed in a set oriented way.

- The processing granularity is an orthogonal dimension with respect to the activation time, both before, after instead of either triggers are either row-level or statement-level. Triggers are all executed in the context of the same transaction to which the triggering operation belongs and also a single trigger activation time is considered. If the monitored event occurs, triggers are all activated immediately after the execution of the triggering transaction.

- The execution order of multiple triggers for the same event is specified using priority with sequential execution of all rules.

The features of triggers supported in various commercial object-relational database systems are described based on the various properties as the following:

- Numbers of events per trigger – Potential events that can lead to the firing of a trigger are inserting, update and delete operations. In DB2 and Informix, a trigger is based on single event. Oracle, MSSQL, Sybase, and Ingres, allow the definitions of a trigger on multiple events on the same table.

- Number of triggers per events – Ingres allows the definition of single trigger for each event. Informix applies the same rule for insert and delete events. In case of update events, multiple triggers are possible if the column lists of the update events are mutually exclusive. The other systems do not have any restrictions with respect to number of triggers per events.

- Trigger granularity – The granularity of a trigger can be FOR EACH ROW or FOR EACH STATEMENT. MSSQL and SYBASE only provide statement-level triggers where as the other systems support both kinds of triggers.

- Transition variables – Within a trigger, transition row variables and transition tables can be referred. In DB2 and Sybase[Any], NEW and OLD are used to refer to the new and old transitions row variables, while NEW TABLE and OLD TABLE are used to the new and old transition tables. MSSQL and SYBASE only provide transition tables, since they only support statement-level triggers. The new and old transition tables are named as INSERTED and DELETED. In Oracle, Informix and Ingres support only transition row variables.

- Trigger activation time – A trigger is fired before or after the specified event is handled. MSSQL, Sybase, and Ingres only provide after triggers, where as the other systems support both kinds of triggers.

- Trigger activation condition – The activation of a trigger is associated with a condition. In DB2, Informix, MSSQL and Sybase the activation condition can be any Boolean SQL expression, and it may even contain subqueries. Oracle and Ingres only allow row-level Boolean SQL expressions that do not contain subqueries.

- Trigger action – In SQL3 and other systems contain the action part of a trigger can be any SQL statement block including SQL data change statements, PL/SQL and procedure calls.

- Execution order of triggers – The execution order is determined by trigger creation timestamp. The execution models of commercial systems are similar to that of SQL3 standard.

- Conflict resolution – A conflict occurs when more than one trigger is fired by an event. DB2, MSSQL, Ingres and Sybase use a creation timestamp based approach to solve rule conflicts. The trigger with the oldest creation timestamp is executed first. Oracle first executes the trigger with the newest creation timestamp and Sybase[Any] requires a user-defined execution order specified using order clause in the trigger definition.

- Trigger inheritance – A trigger is defined on an event that occurs on a parent table can be implicitly triggered by the corresponding event on a subtable. SQL3, DB2 supports trigger inheritance.

6.3.   Classification and Use of Trigger Systems

Classification of Trigger Systems

In general, triggers are classified into following categories based on the function and behavior.

- **Constraint-preserving triggers**: Signal integrity constraint violations and force rollbacks of the violating transactions.
- **Constraint-restoring triggers**: Detect integrity constraint violations and modify the database contents in order to restore integrity.
- **Invalidating triggers**: Signal and mark integrity constraint violations, allowing applications to respond appropriately.
- **Materializing triggers**: Compute materialized derived information from simple scalar values to aggregate values to complex views, either by incremental modifications or complete refresh.
- **Metadata triggers**: Maintain consistency across system catalogs.
- **Replication triggers**: Replicate, migrate, or log information and/or modifications from one table or database (primary copy) to another one (the secondary copy).
- **Extenders**: Manage new types of data (e.g., validate input) and keep specialized external structures consistent with the base data.
- **Alerters**: Notify or push information to users in the form of messages based on publish/subscribe model.
- **Ad-hoc triggers**: Implement business rules, for example supply-chain management or any other application specific logic.

Use of Trigger Systems

Triggers can be used in a variety of significant ways in database systems and applications. The usage of trigger system is characterized by its abstraction level in an information system.

The top level consists of triggers focused on improved user-system interaction and this group is divided into the following categories:

- **User notification**: Certain database situations require user intervention. Triggers are used to detect them automatically and to inform the user.
- **Application procedures**: Triggers are used to create abstraction level for organizing related actions under an event. Upon the occurrence of an event, a series of actions is executed automatically by the trigger system.

- **Default settings**: A recurring application operation is set to defaults. Triggers activated upon database insertions can used for this purpose.
- **Communication**: Triggers offer a medium of communication. Applications can indirectly exchange data through trigger execution. An application causes a trigger to execute, which activates the target application.

The second level consists of triggers aimed at providing the functionality prescribed by a data model and this group is divided into two categories:

- **Integrity enforcement**: Integrity is enforced with triggers and the integrity violation is specified in the condition part of a trigger and the action part specifies the corrective action for the transaction involved.
- **Protection**: Database access is controlled using triggers.

The third level contains triggers used within the kernel of a DBMS itself and their usage is to simplify management of physical resources and complex database states. This group is divided into the following categories:

- **Physical storage optimization**: Triggers are used to adapt the storage structures, access paths, clustering, and check pointing actions and they are defined to maintain statistics for query optimization.
- **View management**: Complex materialized views are easier to maintain with triggers. Whenever the base relations are updated, the materialized view can be updated by calculation of a data change.

Advantages of Triggers

The advantages of triggers are summarized as follows:

- Triggers are reliable since they are automatically invoked whenever an appropriate event is issued by the transaction.
- Monitoring purposes such as monitoring of user accesses and modifications on certain sensitive data.
- Automatic propagation of modifications.
- Enforce complex security authorization.
- Provide auditing and prevent invalid transactions.
- Gather statistics on table access.
- Business rules can easily be enforced by defining triggers, which will automatically be invoked by application programs when necessary.

6.4.   Oracle Triggers

This section illustrates the use of triggers with commercial object-relational database system Oracle. Since the syntax of Oracle triggers are close to the way active rules are specified in the SQL3 standard.

In Oracle, the ECA model is used to specify the active rules. A rule in the ECA model has three components such as event, condition and action. The syntax for specifying triggers in Oracle is shown in Figure 6.5.

A trigger is fired whenever a table is modified by the triggering events such as insert, update, delete.

Once a trigger is fired, it executes SQL statements defined in the trigger action. The reactive behavior is handled in a timely manner using a BEFORE or an AFTER trigger. A BEFORE trigger is activated before the operation modifies the table executed and an AFTER trigger is activated after the modifying operation executes.

Each trigger can access the old value and new values of the changed data by means of transition variables, such as OLD ROW and NEW ROW. The granularity of a trigger is specified as either FOR EACH ROW or FOR EACH STATEMENT, which refers to row-level and statement-level triggers respectively.

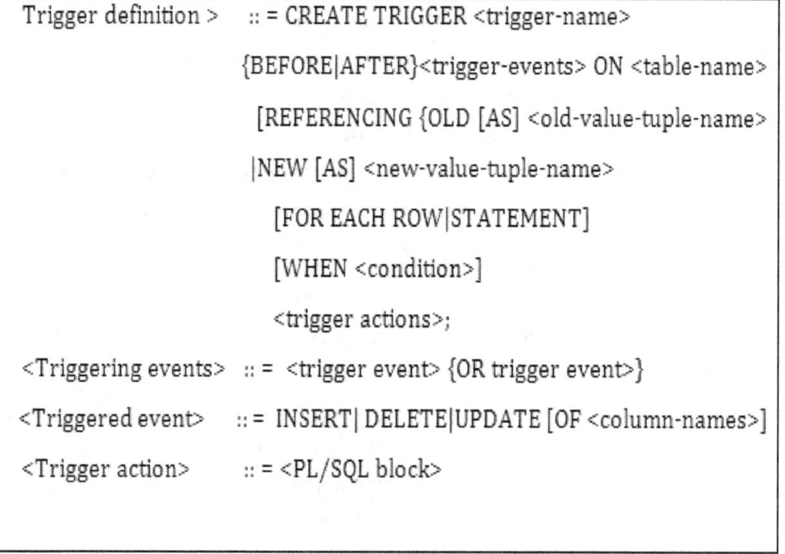

Figure 6.5: Trigger Syntax in Oracle

Let us consider an example database named as COMPANY which consists of two tables such as EMPLOYEE and DEPARTMENT and is shown in Figure 6.6. The EMPLOYEE table contains the details such as employee number (Eno), employee name (Ename), salary (Salary), department to which they are currently assigned (Dno, a foreign key to DEPARTMENT). For this example an employee may be temporarily unassigned to any department and thus NULL is allowed for Dno. Also the DEPARTMENT table has a department name (Dname), department number (Dno), total salary of all employees assigned to the department (Total-salary) and a manager (Manager-no).

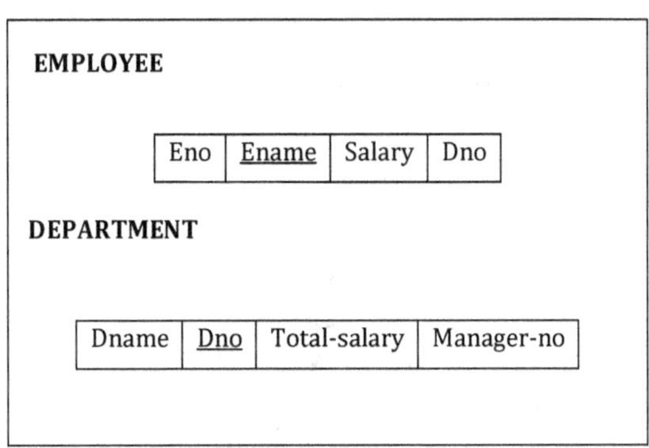

Figure 6.6: Company Database

The Total-salary attribute is a derived attribute whose value should be the sum of the salaries of all employees who are assigned to particular department. Maintaining the correct value of the Total-salary can be monitored using an active rule.

In order to monitor the derived attribute, first the various events that may cause a change in the value of Total-salary are to be determined and the occurrence of events is as follows:

- Inserting one or more new employee records
- Changing the salary of one or more existing employees
- Changing the assignment of existing employees from one department to another
- Deleting one or more employee records

The four triggers R1, R2, R3, and R4 corresponding to the above situation are specified in Figure 6.7. The triggers specified in Figure 6.7 are used to automatically maintain the consistency of total salary (Total-salary) of DEPARTMENT table. The basic events that are specified for triggering rules are the standard SQL update commands such as INSERT, DELETE and UPDATE.

R1: CREATE TRIGGER Total-salary1

    AFTER INSERT ON EMPLOYEE

    FOR EACH ROW

    WHEN (NEW.Dno **IS NOT NULL)**

        UPDATE DEPARTMENT

        SET TOTAL-salary = Total-salary + **NEW**.Salary

        WHERE Dno = **NEW**.Dno;

R2: CREATE TRIGGER Total-salary2

    AFTER UPDATE OF Salary **ON** EMPLOYEE

    FOR EACH ROW

    WHEN (NEW.Dno **IS NOT NULL)**

        UPDATE DEPARTMENT

        SET TOTAL-salary = Total-salary + **NEW**.Salary – **OLD**.Salary

        WHERE Dno = **NEW**.Dno;

R3: CREATE TRIGGER Total-salary3

    AFTER UPDATE OF Dno **ON** EMPLOYEE

    FOR EACH ROW

        BEGIN

        UPDATE DEPARMENT

        SET TOTAL-salary = Total-salary + **NEW**.Salary

        WHERE Dno = **NEW**.Dno;

        UPDATE DEPARMENT

        SET TOTAL-salary = Total-salary - **OLD**.Salary

        WHERE Dno = **OLD**.Dno;   **END;**

R4: CREATE TRIGGER Total-salary4

    AFTER DELETE ON EMPLOYEE

    FOR EACH ROW

    WHEN (OLD.Dno **IS NOT NULL)**

        UPDATE DEPARTMENT

        SET TOTAL-salary = Total-salary – **OLD**.Salary

        WHERE Dno = **OLD**.Dno;

Figure 6.7: Triggers to Maintain the Consistency of Total-Salary of Employee

Rule R1 is triggered, after an INSERT operation is applied to the EMPLOYEE table. In R1, the condition (NEW.Dno IS NOT NULL) is checked and it evaluates to true, (i.e. newly employee record is related to a department) then the action is executed. Here the action updates the DEPARTMENT record(s) related to the newly inserted employee by adding their salary (NEW.Salary) to the Total-salary attribute of their related department.

Rule R2 is triggered by an UPDATE to the Salary attribute of EMPLOYEE table, which updates the salary of an employee. In R2, the condition (NEW.Dno IS NOT NULL) is checked and it evaluates to true, (i.e. newly employee record is related to a department) then the action is executed. Here the action updates the DEPARTMENT record(s) related to the updated salary of an employee by adding the new salary (NEW.Salary) to the Total-salary attribute and also subtracting the old salary (OLD.Salary) form the Total-salary attribute of their related department.

Rule R3 is triggered by an UPDATE to the Dno attribute of EMPLOYEE table, which signifies changing an employee's assignment from one department to another. Here there is no condition check and the action is executed whenever the triggering event occurs. The action updates the both old and new department of the reassigned employees by adding their salary to Total-salary of their new department and subtracting the salary from Total-salary of their old department.

Rule R4 is triggered, after a DELETE operation is applied to the EMPLOYEE table. In R4, the condition (OLD.Dno IS NOT NULL) is checked and it evaluates to true, (i.e. old employee record is related to a department) then the action is executed. Here the action updates the DEPARTMENT record(s) related to the deleted employee by subtracting their salary (OLD.Salary) from the Total-salary attribute of their related department.

The triggers created in Figure 6.7 for COMPANY database are useful for automatically maintaining the consistency of the derived attribute Total-salary of DEPARTMENT table. Since the trigger actions for rules 1, 2 and 4 are to automatically update the values of Total-salary for the employee's department to reflect the newly inserted, updated and deleted employee's salary. However in the case of rule 3, double action is performed. One is, to update the Total-salary of the employee's new department and the other is to update the Total-salary of the employee's old department.

6.5.   Design and Implementation Issues of AORDBS

Active mechanism is useful to monitor and control activities for event-based applications in database systems. Object-relational database systems implement active mechanism in the limited form of triggers which are primarily used to enforce various integrity constraints driven by the application. In order to meet the demands of event-driven and constraint-driven applications in centralized and distributed environments, the development of generic active rule system is required in AORDBS. However the design and implementation of generic active rule system creates various issues related to the specification and processing of active rules in AORDBS which are described as the following.

- **Rule maintenance** – This issue concerns the activation, deactivation and grouping of rules. The activate command can make the rule active again. A deactivated rule cannot trigger by the triggering event. Another facility is to group rules into named rule sets, so that whole set of rules can be activated, deactivated or dropped. In addition to creating rules, the active database system should allow users to insert, update and deleting rules.

- **Rule processing point or Coupling modes** – This issue concerns whether triggered action should be executed before, after or instead of with the triggering event. A before trigger executes the trigger before executing the event that caused the trigger. An after trigger executed the trigger after executes the event. An instead of trigger executed the trigger instead of executing the event. A related issue is whether the action being executed should be considered as a separate transaction or whether should be part of the same transaction that triggered the rule. The rule action is to be executed only after the condition evaluates to true or false. The three possible modes for rule condition evaluation are immediate, deferred and detached. In immediate mode, the condition is evaluated as the part of the same transaction as the triggering event and is evaluated immediately. In the case of deferred mode the condition is evaluated at the end transaction that included the triggering the event. In detached mode, the condition is evaluated as a separate transaction, spawned from the triggering transaction.

- **Rule processing granularity** – It is an issue refers to the aspect of determining how often the system runs the rule evaluation procedure and is defined at different levels such as row-level and statement-level rules. Because SQL update statements can specify a set of rules the user has to distinguish between whether the rule should be considered once for the whole statement or whether it should considered separately for each row affected by the statement.

- **Rule scheduling** – Rule scheduling is an important issue to determine the execution priority and the execution semantics of multiple triggered rules. Whenever an event occurrence causes the triggering of multiple rules at the same time, the rule scheduler should determine the ordering and the execution of rules to be fired for execution. The ordering of next rule to be fired is based on the conflict resolution policies such as dynamic and static priority schemes and the number of rules to be fired for execution by using sequential or concurrent execution of rules.

- **Rule termination** – Termination is an issue to verify that a set of rules is consistent. Termination specifies the action execution of a rule may cause the occurrence of some new events. These new events may in turn, trigger other rules. This could lead to an infinite loop by a chain of triggering. The termination of rule processing is often unpredictable. The use of termination analysis tools can be helpful in highlighting the potential cycles in an active rule set.

- **Easy-to-use tools** – One of the difficulties that may have limited the use of active rules in database systems is that there are no easy-to-use tools for writing, debugging, verifying and monitoring of active rules. It is necessary to develop tools to implement active rules potentially in database applications.

- **Time based triggers** –Activate triggers at time a point reached or after time intervals elapsed is a valuable functionality which requires the temporal extensions in active rules.

Most of the active object-relational database systems do not handle the above issues completely. Research on active object-relational database systems is driven by a need to provide active mechanism effectively for a number of advanced applications, specifically the extension needed to develop the efficient rule processing mechanism in active object-relational database system.

6.6.   Summary

Active rules that specify actions that are triggered by certain events are the important enhancement to database systems. The active object-relational database system supports advanced applications to monitor changes in the database state and to initiate appropriate actions automatically without user intervention. This chapter has explained the knowledge and execution model of SQL3 standard for trigger definition and processing. This chapter also specified the features of triggers in SQL3 standard and also in commercial database systems. This chapter has described the classification and the use of triggers in database systems. This chapter has also illustrated the use of triggers in the object-relational database system using Oracle triggers. Finally this chapter has discussed the several issues related to the design and implementation of generic active rule system in active object-relational database system.

Review Questions

1. What is an SQL trigger?
2. Explain the trigger in SQL3 standard.
3. Write the syntax of SQL3 trigger.
4. Describe the knowledge model of SQL3 standard.
5. Explain the execution model of SQL3 standard.
6. Describe the various features provided by the SQL3 triggers.
7. Write about the different categories of triggers.
8. Describe the various ways of using trigger systems.
9. Write down the advantages of using triggers.
10. Explain the use of triggers in object-relational database system with an example.

References

1. J.A. Bailey and K. Ramamohanarao, "Issues in active databases", In Proceedings of the 6th Australasian Database Conference, Pp. 27-35, 1996.

2. S. Ceri, R.J. Cochrane and J. Widom, "Practical applications of triggers and constraints: Successes and lingering issues", In Proceedings of the 26th International Conference on Very Large Data Bases, Pp. 254- 262, Cairo, Egypt, 2000.

3. R. Cochrane, H. Pirahesh and N. Mattos, "Integrating Triggers and Declarative Constraints in SQL Database Systems", In Proceedings of the 22nd VLDB Conference, Mumbai, India, 1996.

4. K.R. Dittrich and S. Gatziu, "Time Issues in Active Database Systems", In Snodgrass, editor, Proceedings of the International Workshop on an Infrastructure for Temporal Databases, Arlington, Texas, 1993.

5. A. Eisenberg and J. Melton, "SQL: 1999, formerly known as SQL3", SIGMOD Record, Vol. 28, No.1, Pp. 131-138, 1999.

6. R. Elmasri and S. Navathe, "Database Systems: Models, Languages, Design and Application Programming", Sixth edition, Pearson Education Ltd, 2013.

7. K. Kulkarni, N. Mattos and R. Cochrane, "Active database features in sql-3", In N. Paton(ed.), Active Rules in Database Systems, Pp. 197-219, Springer-Verlag, 1999.

8. J.M. Marin, G.P. Lechuga, X. Li and J.C. Mora, "ECA rule analysis in a Distributed Active Database", In Proceedings of the International Conference on Computer Technology and Development, IEEE Computer Society, Pp. 113-116, 2009.

9. M. Schaff, A. Koschel, S.G. Grivas and I. Astrova, "An Active DBMS Style Activity Service for Cloud Environments", The International Conference on Cloud Computing, GRIDs, and Virtualization, Pp. 80-85, IARIA, ISBN: 978-1-61208-106-9, 2010.

10. E. Simon and A.K. Dittrich, "Promises and Realities of Active Database Systems", In Proceedings of the 21st Inter. Conference on Very Large Data Bases, Pp. 642-653, Zurich, Switzerland, 1995.

11. B. Thome, D. Gawlick and M. Pratt, "Event Processing with an Oracle Database", ACM SIGMOD, Pp. 863-867, 2005.

12. C. Turker and M. Gertz, "Semantic integrity support in SQL: 1999 and commercial (object-) relational database management systems", The VLDB Journal, Vol. 10, No. 4, Pp. 241-269, 2001.

13. G. Zhang, D. Deng, Z. Gong and P.C.Y. Sheu, "Active Rule Processing Technology Application for Electronic Commerce", IEEE Computer Society, Pp. 389-393, 2009.

Glossary of Terms

ACID properties – In database systems, transactions have four basic ACID (Atomicity, Consistency, Isolation and Durability) properties which are used to ensure that a database remains stable state after the transaction is executed. The atomicity and durability property is the responsibility of the recovery subsystem of the DBMS. The preservation of consistency is the responsibility of the DBMS and the application developers by enforcing integrity and enterprise constraints. The isolation property is enforced by the concurrency subsystem of the DBMS.

Active database systems – A database system coupled with event-condition-action (ECA) rules is known as the active database system (ADBS) which provides active mechanism to monitor changes in the database state and initiate appropriate actions automatically without user intervention based on the ECA rules stored in the DBMS.

Active object-relational database system – Integration of an active database system with the object-relational database system is commonly referred to as active object-relational database system that extends the normal functionality of the object-relational database system with support to monitor the changes to the database state and react to specific situations automatically without user intervention.

Application programmers – These people implement the specifications specified by the analysts as programs. Application programmers are also called as software engineers should well familiar with all DBMS facilities.

Casual users – These users need different information each time and occasionally access the database. They use sophisticated query language to specify their requests. Casual users need to learn only a few facilities of the DBMS that they use repeatedly.

Client – A client is a user machine that provides user interface capabilities and local processing.

Client/Server architecture – Client and servers are the separate logical entities that are connected over the computer network to perform a specific task.

Conceptual database design – It is the process of constructing a conceptual model of the data used in an organization.

Conceptual data model – A conceptual data model gives the comprehensive view of the entire database. This model provides concepts such as entities, attributes and relationships to model the database based on the many users perceive data. Entity-Relationship (ER) model is the most popular high-level conceptual data model. The ER model is commonly used for the conceptual design of database applications.

Concurrency – Concurrency is a property of a transaction system representing the fact that multiple activities are executed at the same time.

Concurrency control – Concurrency control is a technique which is used to ensure the correctness of the database, whenever a database is shared and updated by multiple transactions concurrently.

Constraints – Constraints are used to define the correctness of the data in the database.

Coupling modes – The rule processing point that specifies the time when a triggered transaction is executed with respect to the triggering transaction or event. The three basic coupling modes are immediate, deferred and detached or decoupled.

Data – Data is a single piece of information. A multiple number of data elements in terms of field value can be stored in the form of a record in a database.

Database – A database is a shared collection of logically related data which is used by several applications or users.

Data abstraction – A database system provides the conceptual representation of data to the users and hides the storage and implementation details of data. Data model is a type of data abstraction that is used to provide the conceptual representation of data to the users.

Database administrator (DBA) – The DBA is the administrator, who is responsible for managing the database resources such as the database and the DBMS software. The DBA is also responsible for authorizing database access to the users, coordinating and monitoring the database use and acquiring software and hardware resources as required. The DBA is accountable for problems such as security threats and poor system response time. In order to carry out these functions, the DBA is assisted by a staff in large organizations.

Data definition language (DDL) – Data definition language allows users to define the database, specify the data types, data structures and the constraints on the data to be stored in the database and it also translates the schema written in a source language into the object schema.

Database design – Database design is the process of creating a design that will support the organization's objectives for the required database system.

Database designer – A Database designer is responsible for identifying the data to be stored in the database and for choosing appropriate structure to represent and store the data. A database designer is also responsible to interact with all perspective of database users and understand their requirements for creating a database design that satisfy the requirements of all user groups.

Data dictionary – Data dictionary is a repository of information about database that documents data elements of a database. Data dictionary is an integral part of DBMS that also store and manages Meta data.

Data independence – Data independence is defined as, the capacity to change the schema at one level of a database system without having to change the schema at the next higher level.

Data integrity – Data integrity refers to correctness and accuracy nature of the stored data.

Data item – Data item is the smallest named unit of data that has meaning in the real world.

Database management system – A database management system (DBMS) is a software system that enables the user to define, store, modify and access the data from a database in a consistent and secured manner.

Database manager – Database manager is the central software component of the DBMS which interfaces with user submitted application programs and queries. The database manager is also called as database control system and it handles database access at runtime with the subcomponents such as authorization control, command processor, integrity checker, query optimizer, transaction manager, scheduler, recovery manager and buffer manager.

Data manipulation language (DML) – Data manipulation language allows users to insert, update, delete and retrieve data from the database and it also provides general query facilities through query language.

Data model –A data model is an abstraction of data that helps in the understanding of the structure of database. The structure of the database implies data types, relationships and constraints that apply to the data. The purpose of building a data model is to organize the data in a database.

Database system – A database system is a database management system together with one or more databases.

Database schema – The description of a database is called as the database schema which is specified during database design.

Database state – The data in the database at a particular moment in time is called a database state or snapshot.

Deferred coupling – In the deferred coupling mode, the triggered transaction is executed at the end of the triggering transaction, but before the commit of the triggering transaction.

Detached or decoupled coupling – In the case of detached coupling mode, the triggered transaction is executed as a separate transaction.

Execution model – Execution model determines the processing of rules at runtime and it captures the runtime characteristics of rule processing includes event detection, signaling of events, scheduling of rules and rule execution.

Entity – A relation schema consists of set of attributes which represents the common properties of a real world object called an entity.

End users – End users are the people whose role is to access the database for getting data. The various categories of end users are casual users, naive users, standalone users and sophisticated users.

Event – An event is a relevant happening that are to be monitored by the active database system. An event is categorized as either primitive or composite.

Event signaling – The event signaling phase detects and signals the occurrence of the event.

File – File is a collection of records of a single type.

Flat transaction model – Transactions that have strict ACID properties with single level structure is called flat transaction model. Flat transaction is not decomposable that either completely runs in isolation and commits or fails and undoes all the changes made on the way. Thus when a transaction fails, flat model provides rollback of the entire transaction.

Immediate coupling – In the immediate coupling mode, the triggered transaction is executed immediately after the event is signaled.

Integrated architecture – In integrated architecture, the active functionality is embedded in the existing conventional database system. In this architecture the kernel or core functionality of the underlying DBMS is enhanced to include situation monitoring, event detection and rule processing.

Knowledge model – Knowledge model is used to define the syntax and specification of ECA rules for describing reactive behavior. The knowledge model describes the structural characteristics of rules such as types of events, context of conditions and actions.

Layered architecture – In layered architecture, the active functionality is implemented on top of an existing database system with no modification to the underlying DBMS. Layered architecture requires that a layer be built, through which all ECA rule specifications are routed.

Logical database design – It is the process of constructing a model of the data used in an organization based on a specific model, but independent of the particular DBMS and other physical considerations.

Metadata – Metadata is the data about data. It is also called system catalog which describes the database structure, constraints, applications, authorization and size of data types.

Middleware – Middleware is software that connects the client to the server for allowing the clients to access data from server.

Naive users – These users constantly query and update the database using standard types of queries to perform their tasks. Naive users need to learn the user interface facilities provided by the DBMS. For example bank tellers and reservation agents are called as the naive users of the database. Bank tellers check account balances and post deposits and withdrawals. Reservation agents check the availability of seats to make reservation.

Object based data models – The object based model consists of static properties such as objects, attributes and relationships and dynamic properties such as operations defining new database states based on applied state changes. The two important object based data models used in the database systems are the object-oriented and object-relational data models.

Object-oriented data model – Object-oriented data model organizes the information in terms of objects, where each object has a number of attributes such as simple values, complex values, references to other objects, or methods.

Object-relational data model – Object-relational data model combines the benefits of both relational and object-oriented data model. This model extends the relational model with the support of object-oriented programming features such as encapsulation, inheritance, class definitions and support for complex unstructured data.

Object-relational database management system – Object-relational database management system (ORDBMS) unifies relational database technology with object-oriented programming concepts through object-relational data model to support the management of complex data for advanced applications.

Physical database design – It is the process of producing the description of the implementation of the database on secondary storage which includes the file organization, indexes used to achieve efficient access to the data and security measures.

Physical data models – Physical data models describe how data is stored in storage media.

Primitive events – Primitive events are atomic events which are associated with a point in time. Primitive events are defined in the system and are classified based on their origin as internal and external. Internal events are associated with the access to the database and the external events are produced by the occurrences outside the database in its environment.

Record – Record is a group of related data items treated as a unit by an application program.

Record based data models – In a record based model, the database consists of a number of fixed format records with different types. Each record type defines a fixed number of fields with a fixed length for each. The three types of record based data model are relational data model, network data model and hierarchical data model.

Relational data model – Relational data model organizes the information in relations using the form of two-dimensional tables.

Relationship – A relationship is an association between two or more entities. The relationship that exists among the entities relates data items to each other in a meaningful way.

Representational data models – Representational data models define the data structure along with the relationships between the data elements. The relationships between data elements can be expressed in many different ways. The various types of representational data models suggested are fall under the category of either record based or object based models.

Rule triggering – The event activates the corresponding active rules in the triggering phase.

Rule scheduling – The rule scheduling phase indicates the order to process the rule conflict set when multiple rules are triggered at the same time.

Standalone users – These users maintain personal databases and use GUI based prewritten packages to perform their tasks. Standalone users need to learn most of the facilities of the DBMS for their use. For example, tax calculation package provides the facility to calculate tax of an employee in an organization.

Scheduler – The scheduler is responsible for controlling concurrent execution of transactions by implementing a specific algorithm for concurrency control. The scheduler is also referred to as lock manager, if the concurrency control algorithm is locking.

Serializability – Serializability is used as a correctness criterion for concurrency control in database applications and it ensures that database transitions from one state to other are based on an interleaved execution of a set of concurrent transactions. Serializability in database systems is guaranteed through the designing of concurrency control algorithms.

Server – A server is a system that provides services to the client machines such as file access, database access and web access.

Sophisticated users – These users are well familiar with the facilities of the DBMS and develop their own applications based on their requirements. Business analysts, engineers, and scientists are the examples of sophisticated users.

Structured query language (SQL) – Structured query language is the standard language for retrieving and manipulating data in relational database systems.

SQL3 – SQL3 is the standard for commercial object-relational database management systems.

SQL3 trigger – A trigger in SQL3 standard is an ECA rule that is activated by a database state transition and SQL3 predicate is a condition and SQL3 statements is an action. A trigger is activated whenever a specified event occurs and the event is usually an INSERT, DELETE, or UPDATE operations on a particular table monitored by the trigger.

System analysts – System analysts determine the requirements of end users and develop specifications for standard transactions. These people should familiar with all capabilities provided by the DBMS.

Three-level architecture – The three different views of the data for providing data abstraction in a database is known as three-level architecture that includes the external, conceptual and internal levels.

Transaction manager – A system that manages transactions and controls their access to a DBMS is called the transaction manager that coordinates transactions on behalf application programs.

Transaction model – A transaction model is basically a set of rules which govern the execution and properties of transactions and it is characterized by transaction structure, object structure and correctness criterion.

Trigger – Trigger is a procedural component that allows database designers to instruct the database system to monitor and perform certain operations automatically, whenever the specified events occur on particular tables in an application.

BIBLIOGRAPHY

1. S. Abiteboul, R. Agrawal, P. Bernstein, M. Carey, S. Ceri, B. Croft, D. DeWitt, M. Franklin, H.G. Molina, D. Gawlick, J. Gray, L. Haas, A. Halevy, J. Hellerstein, Y. Ioannidis, M. Kersten, M. Pazzani, M. Lesk, D. Maier, J. Naughton, H. Schek, T. Sellis, A. Silberschatz, M. Stonebraker, R. Snodgrass, J. Ullman, G. Weikum, J. Widom and S. Zdonik, "The Lowell database research self-assessment", Communications of the ACM, Vol. 48, No. 5, Pp. 111-118, 2005.

2. D. Agarwal, J.L. Bruno, A.E. Aabbadi and V. Krishnaswamy, "Relative serializability: An approach for relaxing the atomicity of transactions", Proceedings of the ACM SIGMOD International Conference on Management of Data, Pp. 139-149, 1994.

3. R. Agrawal, A. Ailamaki, P.A. Bernstein, E.A. Brewer, M.J. Carey, S. Chaudhuri, A. Doan, D. Florescu, M.J. Franklin, H. Garcia- Molina, J. Gehrke, L. Gruenwald, L.M. Haas, A.Y. Halevy, J.M. Hellerstein, Y.E. Ioannidis, H.F. Korth, D. Kossmann, S. Madden, R. Magoulas, B. ChinOoi, T.O. Reilly, R. Ramakrishnan, S. Sarawagi, M. Stonebraker, A.S. Szalay and G. Weikum, "The Claremont Report on Database Research", ACM Communications, Vol. 52, 2009.

4. E. Anwar, L. Maugis and S. Chakravarthy, "A new perspective on rule support for object-oriented databases", ACM SIGMOD Record, Vol. 22, No. 2, Pp. 99-108, 1993.

5. E. Anwar, S. Chakravarthy and M. Viveros, "Realizing Transaction Models: An Extensible Approach using ECA Rules", Technical report UF-CIS-TR-95-029,Computer and Information Science and Engineering Department, University of Florida, Florida, 1995.

6. N.B. Al-Jumah, H.S. Hassanein and M. El-Sharkawi, "Implementation and modeling of two-phase locking concurrency control–a performance study", Information and Software Technology, Elsevier, Vol. 42, No. 4, Pp. 257-273, 2000.

7. J. Bae, H. Bae, S.H. Kang, Y. Kim, "Automatic Control of Workflow Processes Using ECA Rules", IEEE Transactions on Knowledge and Data Engineering, Vol. 16, No. 8, Pp. 1010-1023, 2004.

8. S. Bagui, "Achievements and Weaknesses of Object-Oriented Databases", Journal of Object Technology, Vol. 2, No. 4, Pp. 29-41, 2003.

9. J.A. Bailey and K. Ramamohanarao, "Issues in active databases", In Conference on Proceedings of the 6th Australasian Database, Pp. 27-35, 1996.

10. J. Bailey, D. Dong and K. Ramamohanarao, "On the decidability of the termination problem of active database systems", Theoretical Computer Science, Elsevier, Vol. 311, No. 1-3, Pp. 389-437, 2004.

11. E. Baralis and A. Bianco, "Performance evaluation of rule execution semantics in active databases", In Proceedings of the 13th International Conference on Data Engineering, Pp. 365-374, 1997.

12. N.S. Barghouti and G.E. Kaiser, "Concurrency control in advanced database applications", ACM Computing Surveys, Vol. 23, No. 3, Pp. 269-317, 1991.

13. C. Beeri and T. Milo, "A model for active object oriented database", In Proceedings of the 17th International Conference on Very Large Data Bases, Barcelona, Pp. 337-349, 1991.

14. L.B. Bergholt, J.S. Due, R.T. Hohn, J.L. Knudsen, K.H. Nielsen, T.S. Olesen and E.H. Pedersen, "Database Management Systems: Relational, Object-Relational, and Object-Oriented Data models", Center for Object Technology, COT/4-02-V1.1, Pp. 1-120, 1998.

15. M. Berndtsson and B. Lings, "On Developing Reactive Object-Oriented Databases", Special Issue on Active Databases, Bulletin of the Technical Committee on Data Engineering, IEEE Computer Society, Vol. 15, No.1-4, 1992.

16. M. Berndtsson, "Management of Rules in Object-Oriented Databases", In Proceedings of the Baltic Workshop on National Infrastructure Databases:Problems, Methods and Experiences, Vilnius, Lithuania, Vol. 1, Pp. 78-85, 1994.

17. P.A. Bernstein and N. Goodman, "Multiversion concurrency control-theory and algorithms", ACM Transactions on Database Systems, Vol. 8, No. 4, Pp. 465-483, 1983.

18. P.A. Bernstein and E. Newcomer, "Principles of transaction processing", Second Edition, Morgan Kaufmann Publishers, Elsevier, 2009.

19. P.A. Bernstein, M.L. Brodie, S. Ceri, D.J. DeWitt, M.J. Franklin, H. Garcia-Molina, J. Gray, G. Held, J.M. Hellerstein, H.V. Jagadish, M. Lesk, D. Maier, J.F. Naughton, H. Pirahesh, M. Stonebraker and J.D. Ullman, "The Asilomar Report on Database Research", SIGMOD Record, Vol. 27, No. 4, Pp. 74-80, 1998.

20. B. Berstel, P. Bonnard, F. Bry, M. Eckert and P.L. Patranjan, "Reactive Rules on the Web, Reasoning Web, Lecture Notes in Computer Science", Springer-Verlag, Pp.183-239, 2007.

21. E. Bertino, G. Guerrini and I. Merlo, "Trigger inheritance and overriding in an active object database system", IEEE Transactions on Knowledge and Data Engineering, Vol. 12, No. 4, Pp. 588-608, 2000.

22. B. Bhargava, "Concurrency control in database systems", IEEE Transactions on Knowledge and Data Engineering, Vol. 11, No. 1, Pp. 3-16, 1999.

23. S. Bhushan, R.B. Patel and M. Dave, "A Secure Time-Stamp Based Concurrency Control Protocol for Distributed Databases", Journal of Computer Science, 3(7), Pp. 561-565, 2007.

24. A.D. Birrell, "An introduction to programming with C# threads", Technical Report MSR-TR2005-68, Microsoft Research, Redmond, Pp. 1-39, 2005.

25. A. Bonifati, S. Ceri and S. Paraboschi, "Active rules for XML: A new paradigm for E-services", The VLDB Journal, Vol. 10, No. 1, Pp. 39-47, 2001.

26. M. Bouzeghoub, F. Fabret, F. Llirbat, M. Matulovic and E. Simon, "Active-design: A generic toolkit for deriving specific rule execution models", Rules in Database Systems, Lecture Notes in Computer Science, Vol. 1312, Pp.197-211, 1997.

27. A. Brayner, T. Harder and N. Ritter, "Semantic serializability: A correctness criterion for processing transactions in advanced database applications", Data&Knowledge Engineering, Elsevier, Vol. 31, No. 1, Pp.1-24, 1999.

28. F. Bry, M. Eckert, P.L. Patranjan and I. Romanenko, "Realizing Business Processes with ECA Rules: Benefits, Challenges, Limits", In Proceedings of the 4th International Workshop on Principles and Practice of Semantic Web Reasoning, Lecture Notes in Computer Science, Vol. 4187, Pp. 48-62, 2006.

29. A.P. Buchmann, "Architecture of Active Database Systems", In N.Paton (ed.) Active Rules in Database Systems, Chapter 2, Pp. 29-48, 1999.

30. A.P. Buchmann, J. Zimmermann, J.A. Blakeley and D.L. Wells, "Building an integrated active OODBMS: requirements, architecture and design decisions", In Proceedings of the 11th International Conference on Data Engineering, Taipei, Taiwan, Pp. 117-128, 1995.

31. H. Butuner, "Advantages of Object-Oriented Over Relational Databases on Real-Life Applications", Research Journal of Economics, Business and ICT, ISSN: 2045-3345, Vol. 5, 2012.

32. C. Calero, F. Ruiz, A. Baroni, F.B. Abreu and M. Piattini, "An ontological approach to describe the SQL: 2003 object-relational features", Computer Standards & Interfaces, Elsevier, Vol. 28, No. 6, Pp. 695-713, 2006.

33. J. Campin, N. Paton and M.H. Williams, "Specifying Active Database Systems in an Object-Oriented Framework", International Journal of Software Engineering and Knowledge Engineering, Vol. 7, No. 1, Pp.101-123, 1997.

34. B. Cantrill and J. Bonwick, "Real world concurrency, Communications of the ACM", Vol. 51, No. 11, Pp. 34-39, 2008.

35. M.J. Carey, R. Jauhari and M. Livny, "On transaction boundaries in active databases: a performance perspective", IEEE Transactions on Knowledge and Data Engineering, Vol. 3, No. 3, Pp. 320-336, 1991.

36. M.J. Carey, D.J. DeWitt, J.F. Naughton, M. Asgarian, P. Brown, J.E. Gehrke and D.N. Shah, "The Bucky Object-Relational Benchmark", In Proceedings of the VLDB, Pp. 135-146,1996.

37. S. Ceri, P. Fraternali, S. Paraboschi and L. Tanca, "Active rule management in Chimera", In Active Database Systems: Triggers and Rules for Advanced Database Processing, J. Widom and S. Ceri eds., Morgan-Kaufmann, Pp. 151-176, 1996.

38. S. Ceri, R.J. Cochrane and J. Widom, "Practical applications of triggers and constraints: Successes and lingering issues", In Proceedings of the 26th International Conference on Very Large Data Bases, Pp. 254- 262, Cairo, Egypt, 2000.

39. S. Ceri, C. Gennaro, S. Paraboschi and G. Serazzi, "Effective scheduling of detached rules in active databases", IEEE Transactions on Knowledge and Data Engineering, Vol. 15, No. 1, Pp. 2-13, 2003.

40. U. Cetintemel, J. Zimmermann, O. Ulusoy and A. Buchmann, "OBJECTIVE: a benchmark for object-oriented active database systems", Journal of Systems and Software, Elsevier, Vol. 45, No. 1, Pp. 31-43, 1999.

41. S. Chakravarthy (ed.), "Special Issue on Active Databases, Bulletin of the Technical Committee on Data Engineering", IEEE Computer Society, Vol. 15, No. 1-4, 1992.

42. S. Chakravarthy, "A Comparative Evaluation of Active Relational Databases", Technical Report UF-CIS-TR-93-002, Department of Computer and Information Sciences, University of Florida, Florida, 1993.

43. S. Chakravarthy, "Architectures and monitoring techniques for active databases: An evaluation", Data & Knowledge Engineering, Elsevier, Vol. 16, No. 1, Pp. 1-26, 1995.

44. S. Chakravarthy, "Early active database efforts: a capsule summary", IEEE Transactions on Knowledge and Data Engineering, Vol. 7, No. 6, Pp. 1008-1010, 1995a.

45. S. Chakravarthy, E. Anwar and L. Maugis, "Design and Implementation of Active Capability for an Object-Oriented Database", Technical Report UF-CIS-TR-93-001, Department of Computer and Information Sciences, University of Florida, Florida, 1993.

46. S. Chakravarthy, E. Anwar, L. Maugis and D. Mishra, "Design of Sentinel: an object-oriented DBMS with event-based rules", Information and Software Technology, Elsevier, Vol. 36, No. 9, Pp. 555–568, 1994.

47. S. Chakravarthy, V. Krishnaprasad, E. Anwar and S.K. Kim, "Composite events for active databases: Semantics, contexts and detection", In Proceedings of the 20th International Conference on Very Large Data Bases, Santiago, Chile, Pp. 606-617,1994a.

48. S. Chakravarthy, V. Krishnaprasad, Z. Tamizuddin and R.H. Badani, "ECA Rule Integration into an OODBMS: Architecture and Implementation", Technical Report UF-CIS-TR-94-023, Department of Computer and Information Sciences, University of Florida, Florida, 1994b.

49. S. Chakravarthy and E. Anwar, "Exploiting Active Database Paradigm for Supporting Flexible Transaction Models", Technical Report UF-CIS-TR-95-026, Computer and Information Science and Engineering Department, University of Florida, Florida, 1995.

50. S. Chakravarthy and R. Le, "ECA Rule Support for Distributed Heterogeneous Environments", In Proceedings of the 14th International Conference on Data Engineering, Orlando, Florida, 1998.

51. R. Chandra and A. Seguev, "Active Databases for Financial Applications", In Proceedings of the 4th International Workshop on Research Issues in Data Engineering, Houston, Texas, Pp. 46-52, 1994.

52. P.K. Chrysanthis and K. Ramamritham, "A taxonomy of correctness criteria in database applications", The VLDB Journal, Vol. 5, No. 1, Pp. 85-97, 1996.

53. M. Cilia, "Active Database Management Systems", Idea Group Inc, 2006.

54. M. Cilia and A.P. Buchmann, "An active functionality service for e-business applications", ACM SIGMOD Record, Vol. 31, No. 1, Pp. 24-30, 2002.

55. M. Cilia, C. Bornhovd and A.P. Buchmann, "Moving Active Functionality from Centralized to Open Distributed Heterogeneous Environments", In Proceedings of the 9th International Conference on Cooperative Information Systems, Lecture Notes in Computer Science, Springer, Vol. 2172, Pp. 195-211, 2001.

56. E.E. Cobb, "The impact of object technology on commercial transaction processing", The VLDB Journal, Springer-Verlag, Vol. 6, No. 3, Pp. 173-190, 1997.

57. R. Cochrane, H. Pirahesh and N. Mattos, "Integrating Triggers and Declarative Constraints in SQL Database Systems", In 22nd VLDB Conference on Proceedings of the Mumbai, India, 1996.

58. T.M. Connolly and C.E. Begg, "Database Systems: A Practical Approach to Design, Implementation, and Management", Third Edition, Pearson Education Ltd, 2004.

59. C. Collet, T. Coupaye and T. Svensen, "NAOS: Efficient and Modular Reactive Capabilities in an Object-Oriented Database System", In Proceedings of the 20th International Conference on Very Large Data Bases, San Mateo, Pp. 132-143, 1994.

60. W.R. Cook, R. Greena, P. Linskey, E. Meijer, K. Rugg, C. Russell, B. Walker and C. Wittig, "Objects and Databases: State of the Union in 2006", In companion to the 21st ACM SIGPLAN

Conference on Object-Oriented Programming Systems, Languages and Applications, Pp. 926-928, 2006.

61. T. Coupaye and C. Collet, "Denotational semantics for an active rule execution model", In Proceedings of the 2nd International Workshop on Rules in Database Systems, Lecture Notes in Computer Science, Springer, Vol. 985, Pp. 36-50, 1995.

62. A. Datta and S.H. Son, "A study of concurrency control in real-time, active database systems", IEEE Transactions on Knowledge and Data Engineering, Vol. 14, No. 3, Pp. 465-484, 2002.

63. U. Dayal, B. Blaustein, A. Buchmann, U. Chakravarthy, M. Hsu, R. Ledin, D.R. McCarthy, A. Rosenthal, S. Sarin, M.J. Carey, M. Livny and R. Jauhari, "The HiPAC project: combining active databases and timing constraints", ACM SIGMOD Record, Vol. 17, No. 1, Pp. 51-70, 1988.

64. U. Dayal, E.N. Hanson and J. Widom, "Active Database Systems", In W.Kim, editor, Modern Database Systems: The Object Model, Interoperability, and Beyond, Pp. 434-456, 1994.

65. U. Dayal, M. Hsu and R. Ladin, "A Transaction Model for Long-Running Activities", In Proceedings of the 17th International Conference on Very Large Data Bases, Pp.113-122, Spain, 1991.

66. U. Dayal, M. Hsu and R. Ladin, "Organizing Long-Running Activities with Triggers and Transactions", In Proceedings of the ACM SIGMOD International Conference on Management of Data, Atlantic, Pp. 204-214, 1990.

67. U. Dayal, M. Hsu and R. Ladin, "Business Process Coordination: State of the Art, Trends, and Open issues", In Proceedings of the 27th International Conference on Very Large Data Bases, Roma, Italy, Pp. 3-13, 2001.

68. R.S. Devarkonda, "Object-relational Database Systems - the road ahead", ACM Crossroads, Vol. 7, No. 3, Pp.15-18, 2001.

69. O. Diaz and A. Jaime, "EXACT: an extensible approach to active object- oriented databases", The VLDB Journal, Vol. 6, No. 4, Pp. 282-295, 1997.

70. O. Diaz, N. Paton and P. Gray, "Rule Management in Object Oriented Databases: A Uniform Approach", 17th International Conference on Very Large Data Bases, Pp. 317-326, 1991.

71. G. Dimitoglou and S. Rotenstreich, "Architecture and Algorithms for Distributed Rule Management and Processing", International Journal of Computer Science and Network Security, Vol. 8 No. 8, Pp. 397-404, 2008.

72. H. Ding, G. Trajcevski and P. Scheuermann, "Efficient Maintenance of Continuous Queries for Trajectories", Geoinformatica, Springer, 2007.

73. A.K. Dittrich and E. Simon, "Active Database Systems: Expectations, Commercial Experience, and Beyond, Active Rules in Database Systems", Monographs in Computer Science, Springer, Pp. 367-404, 1999.

74. K.R. Dittrich, S. Gatziu and A. Geppert, "The active database management system manifesto: A rulebase of ADBMS features", In Proceedings of the 2nd International Workshop on Rules in Databases, Lecture Notes in Computer Science, Springer, Vol. 985, Pp. 1-17, 1995.

75. K.R. Dittrich and S. Gatziu, "Time Issues in Active Database Systems", In Snodgrass, editor, Proceedings of the International Workshop on an Infrastructure for Temporal Databases, Arlington, Texas, 1993.

76. K.R. Dittrich, H. Fritschi, S. Gatziu, A. Geppert and A. Vaduva, "SAMOS in Hindsight: Experiences in Building an Active Object-Oriented DBMS", Technical Report 2000.05, Database Technology Research Group, Department of Information Technology, University of Zurich, Zurich, Switzerland, 2000.

77. W. Du and A.K. Elmagarmid, "Quasi serializability: a correctness criterion for global concurrency control in InterBase", In Proceedings of the 15th International Conference on Very Large Databases, Amsterdam, Pp. 347–355, 1989.

78. K. Dube and B. Wu, "A generic approach to computer-based Clinical Practice Guideline management using the ECA Rule paradigm and active databases", International Journal of Technology Management (IJTM), Vol. 47, No. 1/2/3, Pp. 75-95, 2009.

79. K. Dube, B. Wu and J.B. Grimson, "Using ECA Rules in Database Systems to Support Clinical Protocols", Database and Expert Systems Applications, Lecture Notes in Computer Science, Vol. 2453, Pp. 226-235, 2002.

80. K. Dube, B. Wu and J.B. Grimson, "Framework and architecture for the management of event-condition-action (ECA) rule-based clinical protocols", In Proceedings of the 15th IEEE Symposium on Computer-Based Medical Systems, Pp. 288-294, 2002a.

81. A. Eisenberg and J. Melton, "SQL: 1999, formerly known as SQL3", SIGMOD Record, Vol. 28, No. 1, Pp. 131-138, 1999.

82. A. Eisenberg, J. Melton, K. Kulkarni, J.E. Michels and F. Zemke, "SQL: 2003 has been published", SIGMOD Record, Vol. 33, No. 1, Pp. 119-126, 2004.

83. A.K. Elmagarmid, "Transaction Models For Advanced Database Applications", CSD-TR-91-022, Computer Science Technical Reports, Department of Computer Science, Purdue University, 1991.

84. A.K. Elmagarmid, Y. Leu, W. Litwin and M. Rusinkiewiczt, "A Multidatabase Transaction Model for InterBase", In Proceedings of the 16th International Conference on Very Large Data Bases, Pp. 507-518, 1990.

85. R. Elmasri and S. Navathe, "Fundamentals of Database Systems", 6th edition, Pearson Education Ltd, 2011.

86. A.A. El-Sayed, H.S. Hassanein and M.E. El-Sharkawi, "Effects of shaping characteristics on the performance of nested transactions", Information and Software Technology, Elsevier, Vol. 43, No. 10, Pp. 579-590, 2001.

87. J. Eriksson, "Specifying and Managing Rules in an Active Real-Time Database System", CiteSeer X, 1998.

88. F.M. Facca, S. Ceri, J. Armani and V. Demalde, "Building reactive web applications", In Conference on Proceedings of the 14th International World Wide Web, Pp. 1058–1059, 2005.

89. A.A. Farrag and M.T. Ozsu, "Using semantic knowledge of transactions to increase concurrency", ACM Transactions on Database Systems, Vol. 14, No. 4, Pp. 503-525, 1988.

90. G. Feuerlicht, "Database Trends and Directions: Current Challenges and Opportunities", J. Pokorny, V. Snasel, K. Richta (Eds.), Pp. 163-174, ISBN: 978-80-7378-116-3, 2010.

91. G. Feuerlicht, J. Pokorny and K. Richata, "Object-Relational Database Design: Can Your Application Benefit from SQL 2003?", Information Systems Development, Springer, Pp. 957-987, 2009.

92. M. Fotache and C. Strimbei, "Object-Relational Databases: An Area with Some Theoretical Promises and Few Practical Achievements", Communications of the International Business Information Management Association (IBIMA), ISSN: 1943-7765, Vol. 9, Pp. 47-55, 2009.

93. A. Gal and J. Mylopoulos, "Toward Web-based application management systems", IEEE Transactions on Knowledge and Data Engineering, Vol. 13, No. 4, Pp. 683-702, 2001.

94. H. Garcia-Molina and K. Salem, " Sagas", In Proceedings of the ACM SIGMOD International Conference on Management of Data, Pp. 249-259, 1987.

95. H. Garcia-Molina, D. Gawlik, J. Klein, K. Kleissner and K. Salem, "Modeling long-running activities as nested sagas", IEEE Bulletin of the Technical Committee on Data Engineering, Vol. 14, No. 1, Pp. 14-18, 1991.

96. J.C. Garcia and P. Ferreira, "Concurrency control for distributed cooperative engineering applications", In Proceedings of the ACM Symposium on Applied Computing, Pp. 958-963, 2002.

97. M.O. Garcia, K.R. Braghetto, C. Pu and J.E. Ferreira, "An Implementation of a Transaction Model for Business Process Systems", Journal of Information and Data Management, Vol. 3, No. 3, Pp. 271-286, 2012.

98. S. Gatziu and K.R. Dittrich, "Events in an Active Object-Oriented Database System", In Proceedings of the 1st International Workshop on Rules in Database Systems, Edinburgh, Pp. 23-39, 1993.

99. S. Gatziu and K. Dittrich, "SAMOS: An Active Object-Oriented Database System", Special Issue on Active Databases, Bulletin of the Technical Committee on Data Engineering, IEEE Computer Society, Vol. 15, No. 1-4, 1992.

100. S. Gatziu and K.R. Dittrich, "Detecting Composite Events in Active Databases Using Petri Nets", In proceedings of the 4th International Workshop on Research Issues in Data Engineering: Active Database Systems, Pp. 2-9, 1994.

101. S. Gatziu, A. Geppert and K.R. Dittrich, "Integrating active concepts into an object-oriented database system", In Proceedings of the 3rd International Workshop on Database Programming Languages, Greece, Pp. 399-414, 1991.

102. S. Gatziu, A. Geppert and K.R. Dittrich, "The SAMOS Active DBMS Prototype", Technical Report 94.16, Institute for Informatics, University of Zurich, 1994.

103. S. Gatziu, A. Koschel, G. Von Bultzingsloewen and H. Fritschi, "Unbundling active functionality", ACM SIGMOD Record, Vol. 27, No. 1, Pp. 35-40, 1998.

104. N. Gehani and H.V. Jagadish, "Ode as an Active Database: Constraints and Triggers", 17th International Conference on Very Large Data Bases, Barcelona, Spain, Pp. 327-336, 1991.

105. N.H. Gehani, H.V. Jagadish, O. Shmueli, "Event specification in an active object-oriented database", In Proceedings of the ACM SIGMOD International Conference on Management of Data, San Diego, Pp.81-90, 1992.

106. N.H. Gehani, H.V. Jagadish and O. Shmueli, "Composite Event Specification in Active Databases: Model & Implementation", In Proceedings of the 18th International Conference on Very Large Data Bases, British Columbia, Canada, Pp. 327-338, 1992a.

107. A. Geppert, S. Gatziu and K.R. Dittrich, "Rulebase Evolution in Active Object-Oriented Database Systems: Adapting the Past to Future Needs", Technical Report 95.13, Institute for Informatics, University of Zurich, Zurich, Switzerland, 1995.

108. A. Geppert, S. Gatziu, K.R. Dittrich, H. Fritschi and A. Vaduva, "Architecture and Implementation of the Active Object-Oriented Database Management System SAMOS", Technical Report 95.29, Institute for Informatics, University of Zurich, Switzerland,1995a.

109. A. Geppert, M. Berndtsson, D. Lieuwen and C. Roncancio, "Performance Evaluation of Object-Oriented Active Database Management Systems Using the BEAST Benchmark", Theory and Practice of Object Systems, Vol. 4, No. 3, Pp. 135-149, 1998.

110. C. Godart, "COO: A transaction model to support cooperating software developers Coordination", In Proceedings of the 4th European Software Engineering Conference, Lecture Notes in Computer Science, Springer, Vol. 717, Pp. 361-379, 1993.

111. D. Goldin, S. Srinivasa and V. Srikanti, "Active Databases as Information Systems", In Proceedings of the International Database Engineering and Applications Symposium, Pp. 123-130, 2004.

112. J. Gray, "The Next Database Revolution", In Proceedings of the ACM SIGMOD International Conference on Management of Data, Paris, Pp. 1-4, 2004.

113. J. Grimson, G. Stephens, B. Jung, W. Grimson, D. Berry and S. Pardon, "Sharing health-care records over the Internet", IEEE Internet Computing, Vol. 5, No. 3, Pp. 49-58, 2001.

114. T.K. Haapasalo, I.M. Jaluta, S.S. Sippu and E.O. Soisalon-Soininen, "Concurrency control and recovery for multiversion database structures", In Proceedings of the 2nd PhD Workshop on Information and Knowledge Management, Pp.73-80, 2008.

115. E.N. Hanson, "The Design and Implementation of the Ariel Active Database Rule System", IEEE Transactions on Knowledge and Data Engineering, Vol. 8, No. 1, Pp. 157-153, 1996.

116. E.N. Hanson and J. Widom, "Rule processing in active database systems", International Journal of Expert Systems, Special issue on AI and databases, Vol. 6, No. 1, Pp. 83-119, 1993.

117. T. Harder and K. Rothermel, "Concurrency control issues in nested transactions", The VLDB Journal, Vol. 2, No. 1, Pp. 39-74, 1993.

118. T. Harder, H. Loeser and N. Zhang, "Supporting Adaptable Technical Information Systems in Heterogeneous Environments-Using WWW and ORDBMS", In Proceedings of the 8th International Workshop on Database and Expert Systems Applications, Pp. 295-303, 1997.

119. T. Heimrich and G. Specht, "Enhancing ECA rules for Distributed Active Database Systems", Web Databases and Web Services, LNCS 2593, Springer-Verlag, Pp. 199-205, 2003.

120. J.M. Hellerstein, M. Stonebraker and J. Hamilton, "Architecture of a Database System", Foundations and Trends in Databases, Vol. 1, No. 2, Pp. 141-259, 2007.

121. A. Hinze, K. Sachs and A. Buchmann, "Event-Based Applications and Enabling Technologies", ACM 2009.

122. T. Hong, "A survey of active database systems", In Proceedings of 3rd International Workshop Rules in Database Systems, Lecture Notes in Computer Science, Vol. 1312, 1997.

123. S.L. Hung and K.Y. Lam, "Performance Comparison of Static vs. Dynamic Two Phase Locking Protocols", Journal of Database Administration, Vol. 3, No. 2, Pp. 12-23, 1992.

124. M. Jackson, "Thirty years (and more) of databases", Information and Software Technology, Elsevier, Vol. 41, No. 14, Pp. 969-978, 1999.

125. H.V. Jagadish, A.O. Mendelzon and I.S. Mumick, "Managing Conflicts between Rules", Journal of Computer and System Sciences, Vol. 58, No.1, Pp. 13-28, 1999.

126. Y. Jiang, J. Li and S. Nishimura, "A general stochastic model for dynamic locking in database systems", IEEE Transactions on Computers, Vol. 53, No. 3, Pp. 308-319, 2004.

127. Y. Jin, "A design pattern for active rule-based system architectures", In IEEE International Conference on Information Reuse and Integration, Pp. 536-541, 2005.

128. Y. Jin, "Management of composite event for active database rule scheduling", IEEE International Conference on Information Reuse and Integration, Pp. 300-304, 2009.

129. Y. Jin, S.D. Urban and S.W. Dietrich, "A concurrent rule scheduling algorithm for active rules", Data & Knowledge Engineering, Elsevier, Vol. 60, No. 3, Pp. 530-546, 2007.

130. J.Y. Jung, J. Park, S.K. Han and K. Lee, "An ECA-based framework for decentralized coordination of ubiquitous web services", Information and Software Technology, Elsevier, Vol. 49, No. 11-12, Pp. 1141-1161, 2007.

131. P. Kangsabanik, D.S. Yadav, R. Mall and A.K. Majumdar, "Performance analysis of long-lived cooperative transactions in active DBMS", Data& Knowledge Engineering, Elsevier, Vol. 62, No. 3, Pp. 547-577, 2007.

132. P. Kangsabanik, R. Mall and A.K. Majumdar, "Semantic Based Concurrency Control of Open Nested Transactions in Active Object Oriented Database Management Systems", Distributed and Parallel Databases, Kluwer Academic Publishers, Vol. 8, No. 2, Pp. 181-222, 2000.

133. V. Kantere, M. Manoubi, I. Kiringa, T. Sellis and J. Mylopoulos, "Peer coordination through distributed triggers", In Procd. of the VLDB Endowment, Vol.3, No. 2, Pp. 1561-1564, 2010.

134. V. Kantere and A. Tsois, "Using ECA rules to implement mobile query agents for fast-evolving pure P2P networks", In Proceedings of the 3rd International Joint Conference on Autonomous Agents and Multiagent Systems, Pp. 1510-1511, 2004.

135. R. Kalantari and C.H. Bryant, "Comparing the Performance of Object and Object-Relational Database Systems on Objects of Varying Complexity", Data Security and Security Data, Lecture Notes in Computer Science, Springer, Vol. 6121, Pp. 72-83, 2012.

136. G. Kappel and W. Retschitzegger, "The Trigs active object-oriented database system-an overview", ACM SIGMOD record, Vol. 27, No. 3, Pp. 36-41, 1998.

137. G. Kappel, S.R. Schott and W. Retschitzegger, "Rule Patterns for Designing Active Object-Oriented Database Applications", Technical Report TR-07/95, Department of Information Systems, University of Linz, Austria, 1995.

138. G. Kappel, S.R. Schott and W. Retschitzegger, "Beyond Coupling Modes: Implementing Active Concepts on Top of a Commercial OODBMS", In Proceedings of the International Symposium on Object-Oriented Methodologies and Systems, Lecture Notes in Computer Science, Vol. 858, Pp. 189-204, 1994.

139. G. Kappel, S.R. Schott and W. Retschitzegger, "A Tour on the TriGs Active Database System-Architecture and Implementation", Technical Report, Department of Information Systems, Johannes Kepler University, Linz, 1997.

140. G. Kappel, S.R Schoot, W. Retschitzegger, A.M. Tjoa, S. Vieweg and R. Wagner, "Active object-oriented database systems for CIM applications", In Information Management in Computer Integrated Manufacturing, Lecture Notes in Computer Science, Vol. 973, Pp. 96-131, 1995.

141. G. Kappel, S.R. Schott, W. Retschitzegger and M. Sakkinen, "A Transaction Model For Handling Composite Events", In Proceedings of the 3rd International Workshop of the Moscow ACM SIGMOD on Advances in Databases and Information Systems, 1996a.

142. G. Kappel, S.R. Schott, W. Retschitzegger and M. Sakkinen, "Multi-Parent Subtransactions Covering the Transactional Needs of Composite Events", In International Workshop on Advanced Transaction Models and Architectures, Pp. 269-282, 1996b.

143. N. Kerdprasop, S. Pilabutr and K. Kerdprasop, "Improving Medical Database Consistency with Induced Trigger Rules", New Advances in Intelligent Decision Technologies, Studies in Computational intelligence, Springer-Verlag, Vol. 199, Pp. 265–274, 2009.

144. W. Kim, "Research Directions in Object-Oriented Database Systems", In Proceedings of the 9th ACM SIGACT-SIGMOD-SIGART Symposium on Principles of Database Systems, Pp. 1-15, 1990.

145. W. Kim, "Object-Oriented Database Systems: Promises, Reality and Future", In Proceedings of the 19th International Conference on Very Large Data Bases, Dublin, Ireland, Pp. 676-687, 1993.

146. W. Kim, "Object-Relational - The unification of object and relational database technology", Uni SQL White Paper, 1996.

147. S.K. Kim and S. Chakravarthy, "A Confluent Rule Execution Model for Active Databases", Technical Report UF-CIS-TR-95-032, Computer and Information Science and Engineering Department, University of Florida, Florida, 1995.

148. S.K. Kim and S. Chakravarthy, "A Practical Approach to Static Analysis and Execution of Rules in Active Databases", In Proceedings of the 6th International Conference on Information and Knowledge Management, Pp. 161-168, 1997.

149. P. Konana and Sudha Ram, "Transaction management mechanisms for active and real-time databases: A comprehensive protocol and a performance study", Journal of Systems and Software, Elsevier, Vol. 42, No. 3, Pp. 205-225, 1998.

150. H.F. Korth and G. Speegle, "Formal model of correctness without serializability", In Proceedings of the ACM SIGMOD International Conference on Management of Data, Pp. 379-386, 1988.

151. V. Krishnaswamy, D. Agarwal, J.L. Bruno and A. El Aabbadi, "Relative Serializability: An Approach for Relaxing the Atomicity of Transactions", Journal of Computer and System Sciences, Elsevier, Vol. 55, No. 2, Pp. 344-354, 1997.

152. K. Kulkarni, N. Mattos and R. Cochrane, "Active database features in sql-3", In N. Paton(ed.), Active Rules in Database Systems, Springer-Verlag, Pp. 197-219, 1999.

153. M. Kumar, "Issues and Challenges in Database Research", Global Journal of Computer Science and Technology Software & Data Engineering, Vol. 12, No. 11, 2012.

154. K.I. Kwon and S. Moon, "Semantic multi granularity locking and its performance in object-oriented database systems", Journal of Systems Architecture, Elsevier, Vol. 44, No. 12, Pp. 917-935, 1998.

155. LatifaBaba-hamed and Hafida Belbachir, "The Priority of Rules and the Termination Analysis Using Petri Nets", The International Arab Journal of Information Technology, Vol. 4, No. 2, Pp. 177-183, 2007.

156. S.Y. Lee and R.L. Liou, "A multi-granularity locking model for concurrency control in object-oriented database systems", IEEE Transactions on Knowledge and Data Engineering, Vol. 8, No. 1, Pp. 144-156, 1996.

157. S. Lee, S.J. Kim, W. Kim, The BORD Benchmark for Object-Relational Databases, Database and Expert Systems Applications, Lecture Notes in Computer Science, Pp. 6-20, 2000.

158. N. Leavitt, "Whatever Happened to Object-Oriented Databases?", IEEE Computer, Vol. 33, No. 8, Pp. 16-19, 2000.

159. D. Lomet (ed.), Special Issue on Active Databases, Bulletin of the Technical Committee on Data Engineering, IEEE Computer Society, Vol. 15, No. 1-4, 1992.

160. A. Maatuk, M. Akhtar Ali and N. Rossita, "Converting Relational Databases into Object-relational Databases", In Journal of Object Technology, Vol. 9, No. 2, Pp. 154-161, 2010.

161. S.K. Madria, "A Study of the Concurrency Control and Recovery Algorithms in Nested Transaction Environment", The Computer Journal, Vol. 40, No. 10, Pp. 630-639, 1997.

162. L.V. Mancini, I. Ray, S. Jajodia and E. Bertino, "Flexible Transaction Dependencies in Database Systems", Distributed and Parallel Databases, Kluwer Academic Publishers, Vol. 8, No. 4, Pp. 399-446, 2000.

163. J.M. Marin, G.P. Lechuga, X. Li and J.C. Mora, "ECA rule analysis in a Distributed Active Database", In Proceedings of the International Conference on Computer Technology and Development, IEEE Computer Society, Pp. 113-116, 2009.

164. D.R. McCarthy and U. Dayal, "The architecture of an active database management system", In Proceedings of the ACM SIGMOD International Conference on Management of Data, Portland, Oregon, Pp. 215-224, 1989.

165. S. McClure, "Object Database vs. Object-Relational Databases", International Data Corporation (IDC) Bulletin, 1997.

166. S. Mehrotra, R. Rastogi, H.F. Korth and A. Silberschatz, "Ensuring consistency in multi databases by preserving two-level serializability", ACM Transactions on Database Systems, Vol. 23, No. 2, Pp. 199-230, 1998.

167. S. Meenakshi and V. Thiagarasu, "Correctness Criteria for Transaction Processing: A Survey and Analysis", International Journal of Applied Research & Studies, Vol. I, No. I, 2012.

168. S. Meenakshi and V. Thiagarasu, "Constructive Review of Transaction Models in Database Systems", International Journal of Advanced Research in Computer Science, Vol. 4, No. 4, Pp. 351-356, 2013.

169. S. Meenakshi and V. Thiagarasu, "Design of Rule Scheduler for Trigger Rule Conflict in Active Object-Relational Database Systems", International Journal of Emerging Technologies in Computational and Applied Sciences, ISSN (O): 2279-0055, ISSN(P): 2279-0047, Vol. 2, No. 7, Pp. 185-189, 2014.

170. S. Meenakshi and V. Thiagarasu, "Development of Rule Scheduler for Multiple Triggered Rules in Active Object-Relational Database Systems", International Journal of Innovative Research in Computer and Communication Engineering, ISSN(O): 2320-9801, ISSN(P): 2320-9798, Vol. 2, No. 5, Pp. 4289-4294, 2014.

171. D. Montesi and R. Torlone, "Analysis and optimization of active databases, Data & Knowledge Engineering", Elsevier, Vol. 40, No. 3, Pp. 241-271, 2002.

172. J.E.B. Moss, "Nested Transactions: An Approach to Reliable Distributed Computing", Massachusetts Institute of Technology Press, Cambridge, England, 1985.

173. B. Mukherjee, S. Sengupta and R. Dasgupta, "Application of CTPN Model of Distributed Active Database in Ambient Intelligent Pervasive Computing Environment", International Journal of Systems Applications, Engineering & Development, Vol. 6, No. 6, Pp. 384-391, 2012.

174. F. Najafabadi, H. Reza and A.H. Navin, "Rule scheduling methods in active database systems: A brief survey", In Proceedings of the 6th International Conference on Application of Information and Communication Technologies, Pp. 1-5, 2012.

175. S.B. Navathe, A. Tanaka and S. Chakravarthy, "Active Database Modeling and Design Tools: Issues, Approach and Architecture", In Special Issue on Active Databases, Bulletin of the Technical Committee on Data Engineering, IEEE Computer Society, Vol. 15, No. 1-4, Pp. 6-9, 1992.

176. M.H. Nodine and S.B. Zdonik, "Cooperative transaction hierarchies: Transaction support for design applications", The VLDB Journal, Vol. 1, No. 1, Pp. 41-80, 1992.

177. E. Pardede, J.W. Rahayu and D. Taniar, "New SQL Standard for Object-Relational Database Applications", In Proceedings of the IEEE Conference on Standardization and Innovation of Information Technology, Pp. 191-203, 2003.

178. N.W. Paton and O. Diaz, "Active database systems, ACM Computing Surveys", Vol. 31, No. 1, Pp. 63-103, 1999.

179. N.W. Paton, J. Campin, A.A.A. Fernandes and M.H. Williams, "Formal Specification of Active Database Functionality: A Survey", In T. Sellis, editor, Proceedings of the 2nd International Workshop on Rules in Database Systems, Pp. 21-35, 1995.

180. P. Picouet and V. Vianu, "Semantics and expressiveness issues in active databases", In Proceedings of the 14th ACM SIGACT-SIGMOD-SIGART Symposium on Principles of Database Systems, Pp. 126-138, 1995.

181. P. Picouet and V. Vianu, "Expressiveness and complexity of active databases", Lecture Notes in Computer Science, Springer, Vol. 1186, Pp. 155-172, 1997.

182. P.F. Pires, M.R.F. Benevides and M. Mattoso, "Building Reliable Web Services Compositions", Web, Web-Services, and Database Systems, Lecture Notes in Computer Science, Vol. 2593, Pp. 59-72, 2003.

183. J. Pokorny, "Database architectures: Current trends and their relationships to environmental data management", Environmental Modelling & Software, Elsevier, Vol. 21, No. 11, Pp. 1579-1586, 2006.

184. W.J. Premerlani, M.R. Blaha, J.E. Rumbaugh and T.A. Varwig, "An Object-Oriented Relational Database", Communications of the ACM, Vol. 33, No. 11, Pp. 99-109, 1990.

185. C. Pu, G. Kaiser and N. Hutchinson, "Split-transactions for open-ended activities", In Proceedings of the 14th International Conference on Very Large Data Bases, Pp. 26-37, 1988.

186. B. Purimetla, R.M. Sivasankaran, J.A. Stankovic, K. Ramamritham and D. Towsely, "A study of distributed real-time active database applications", In Proceedings of the IEEE Workshop on Parallel and Distributed Real-Time Systems, Vol. 75, 1993.

187. S. Rabah, J. Li, M. Liu and Y. Lai, "Comparative Studies of 10 Programming Languages within 10 Diverse Criteria", COMP6411-S10 Term Report, arXiv preprint arXiv: 1009.0305, arxiv.org, 2010.

188. K. Rabuzin, M. Malekovic and A. Lovrencic, "The Theory of Active Databases vs. The SQL Standard", In Proceedings of 18th International Conference on Information and Intelligent Systems, Varazdin, Croatia, Pp. 49-54, 2007.

189. K. Rabuzin, M. Baca and M. Malekovic, "A Multimodal Biometric System Implemented within an Active Database Management System", Journal of Software, Academy publisher, Finland, Vol. 2, No. 4, Pp, 24-31, 2007a.

190. K. Rabuzin, M. Malekovic and M. Baca, "A Multimodal Biometric System Based upon the Active Database Paradigm", Journal of Management, Informatics and Human Resources, Slovenia, Vol. 39, No. 7, Pp. 425-431, 2006.

191. K. Rabuzin and M. Malekovic, "Implementing business rules in active databases", In Proceedings of 15th Conference on Information and Intelligent Systems, Pp. 3-9, 2004.

192. J. W. Rahayu, E. Chang, T.S. Dillon and D. Taniar, "Performance evaluation of the object-relational transformation methodology", Data & Knowledge Engineering, Vol. 38, No. 3, Pp. 265-300, 2001.

193. K. Ramamritham and C. Pu, "A formal characterization of epsilon serializability", In IEEE Transaction on Knowledge and Data Engineering, Vol. 7, No. 6, Pp. 997-1007, 1995.

194. K. Ramamritham and P.K. Chrysanthis, "A taxonomy of correctness criteria in database applications", The VLDB Journal, Vol. 5, No. 1, Pp. 85-97, 1996.

195. R. Ramakrishnan and J.Gehrke, "Database Management Systems", second Edition, McGrawHill, 2000.

196. L. Raschid, T. Sellis and A. Delis, "A simulation-based study on the concurrent execution of rules in a database environment", Jour. of Parallel and Distributed Computing, Vol. 20, No. 1, Pp. 20-42, 1994.

197. A. Rasoolzadegan, R. Alesheykh and A. Abdollahzadeh, "A new approach for event triggering probability estimation in active database systems to rule scheduling improvement", In Proceedings of the 2nd IEEE International Conference on Information and Communication Technologies, Vol. 2, Pp. 2920-2925, 2006.

198. A. Rasoolzadegan and M.R. Meybodi, "Rule Scheduling in Active Database Using Learning Automata", International Journal of Computer, Mathematical Sciences and Applications, Serials Publications, Vol. 4, No. 1-2, Pp. 239-262, 2010.

199. A. Reuter, "Databases: The Integrative Force in Cyberspace", Data Management in a Connected World, Lecture Notes in Computer Science, Vol. 3551, Pp. 3-16, 2005.

200. A. Reuter and H. Waechter, "The Contract Model", Data Engineering Journal, Vol. 14, No. 1, Pp. 39-43, 1991.

201. M. Rusinkiewicz, W. Klas, T. Tesch, J. Wasch and P. Muth, "Towards A Cooperative Transaction Model - The Cooperative Activity Model", In 21st International Conference on Very Large Data Bases, Zurich, Switzerland, Pp. 194-205, 1995.

202. Y. Saygin, O. Ulusoy and S. Chakravarthy, "Concurrent rule execution in active databases", Information Systems, Elsevier, Vol. 23, No. 1, Pp. 39-64, 1998.

203. J. Schiefer, S. Rozsnyai, C. Rauscher and G. Saurer, "Event-driven rules for sensing and responding to business situations", In International Conference on proceedings of the ACM Distributed event-based systems, Pp. 198-205, 2007.

204. H. Schuldt, G. Alonso and H.J. Schek, "Concurrency control and recovery in transactional process management", In Proceedings of the 18th ACM SIGMOD-SIGACT-SIGART symposium on Principles of Database Systems, Pp. 316-326, 1999.

205. M. Schaff, A. Koschel, S.G. Grivas and I. Astrova, "An Active DBMS Style Activity Service for Cloud Environments", The International Conference on Cloud Computing, GRIDs, and Virtualization, IARIA, Pp. 80-85, 2010.

206. H. Schuldt, G. Alonso, C. Beeri and H.J. Schek, "Atomicity and isolation for transactional processes", ACM Transactions on Database Systems, Vol. 27, No. 1, Pp. 63-116, 2002.

207. A. Sheth, Y. Leu and A.K. Elmagarmid, "Maintaining Consistency of Interdependent Data in Multidatabase Systems", Technical Report CSD-TR-91-016, 1991.

208. A. Silberschatz and S. Zdonik, "Strategic Directions in Database Systems: Breaking Out of the Box", ACM computing Surveys, Vol. 28, No. 4, Pp. 764-778, 1996.

209. A. Silberschatz, M. Stonebraker and J. Ullman, "Database Research: Achievements and Opportunities into the 21st Century", Report of an NSF Workshop on the Future of Database

Systems Research, Pp. 26-27, 1995.

210. E. Simon and A.K. Dittrich, "Promises and Realities of Active Database Systems", In Proceedings of the 21st International Conference on Very Large Data Bases, Zurich, Switzerland, Pp. 642-653, 1995.

211. R.M. Sivasankaran, J.A. Stankovic, D. Towsley, B. Purimetla and K. Ramamritham, "Priority assignment in real-time active databases", The VLDB Journal, Vol. 5, No. 1, Pp. 19-34, 1996.

212. M. Stonebraker, "The integration of rule systems and database systems", IEEE Transactions on Knowledge and Data Engineering, Vol. 4, No. 5, Pp. 415-423, 1992.

213. M. Stonebraker and G. Kemnitz, "The POSTGRES next-generation database management system", Communications of the ACM, Vol. 34, No. 10, Pp. 78-92, 1991.

214. M. Stonebraker, S. Madden and P. Dubey, "Intel "Big Data" Science and Technology Center Vision and Execution Plan", SIGMOD Record, Vol. 42, No.1, Pp. 44-49, 2013.

215. M. Stonebraker, P. Brown and D. Moore, "Object-Relational DBMSs - Tracking the Next Great Wave", 2nd ed., Morgan Kaufmann, 1999.

216. M. Stonebraker, L.A. Rowe, B.G. Lindsay, P.A. Bernstein, J. Gray, M.J. Carey, M.L. Brodie and D. Beech, "Third-generation database system manifesto", ACM SIGMOD Record, Vol. 19, No. 3, Pp. 31-44, 1990.

217. Y.C. Tay, "Issues in modeling locking performance", Stochastic Analysis of Computer and Communication Systems, Elsevier Science Publishers, Pp. 631-658, 1990.

218. A. Thomasian, "Concurrency control: methods, performance, and analysis", ACM Computing Surveys, Vol. 30, No. 1, Pp. 70-119, 1998.

219. B. Thome, D. Gawlick and M. Pratt, "Event Processing with an Oracle Database", ACM SIGMOD, Pp. 863-867, 2005.

220. C. Turker and M. Gertz, "Semantic integrity support in SQL: 1999 and commercial (object-) relational database management systems", The VLDB Journal, Vol. 10, No. 4, Pp. 241-269, 2001.

221. S. Varde, "Challenging research issues in data mining", databases and information retrieval, ACM SIGKDD Explorations Newsletter, Vol. 11, No. 1, Pp. 49-52, 2009.

222. S. Viana, J.R. Almeida Junior and J. Pavon, "A Rule Repository for Active Database Systems", CLEI ELECTRONIC JOURNAL, Vol. 10, No. 2, Pp. 4, 2007.

223. S. Viana, J. Pavon and J.R. Almeida Junior, "Rule Management in Active Database Systems", In 15th International Conference Proceedings of the on Computing, Mexico, IEEE Computer Society, Pp. 315-322, 2006.

224. G. von Bulltzingsloewen, A. Koschel, P.C. Lockemann and H.D. Walter, "ECA Functionality in a Distributed Environment", Active Rules in Database Systems, Monographs in Computer Science, Springer, Pp. 147-175, 1999.

225. H. Waechter and A. Reuter, "The ConTract Model", In A.K. Elmagarmid (ed.) Database Transaction Models for Advanced Applications, Morgan Kaufmann, San Mateo, Calif., Pp. 217-263, 1992.

226. Wai Yin Mok, "Designing nesting structures of user-defined types in object-relational databases", Information and Software Technology, Elsevier, Vol. 49, Pp. 1017-1029, 2007.

227. C.F. Wai Yin Mok and C.D. Hickman, "Allport, Implementing Business Processes: A Database Trigger Approach", International Journal of Knowledge-Based Organizations, Vol. 3, No. 2, Pp. 36-55, 2013.

228. T. Wang, J. Vonk, B. Kratz and P. Grefen, "A survey on the history of transaction management: from flat to grid transactions", Distributed Parallel Databases, Vol. 23, Pp. 235-270, 2008.

229. D. Wang, E.A. Rundensteiner, H. Wang and R.T. Ellison, "Active Complex Event Processing: Applications in Real-Time Health Care", In Proceedings of the VLDB Endowment, Vol. 3, No. 2, Pp. 1545-1548, 2010.

230. S. Wasserkrug, A. Gal, O. Etzion and Y. Turchin, "Efficient Processing of Uncertain Events in Rule-Based Systems", IEEE Transactions on Knowledge and Data Engineering, Vol. 24, No. 1, Pp. 45-58, 2012.

231. G. Weikum and H.J. Schek, "Concepts and applications of multilevel transactions and open nested transactions", In A.K. Elmagarmid (ed.), Database Transaction Models for Advanced Applications, Morgan Kaufmann, Pp. 350-397, 1992.

232. J. Widom and S.J. Finkelstein, "Set-Oriented Production Rules in Relational Database Systems", In Proceedings of the ACM SIGMOD International Conference on Management of Data, Atlantic City, New Jersey, Pp. 259-270, 1990.

233. J. Widom, "The Starburst Rule System: Language Design, Implementation, and Applications", Special Issue on Active Databases, Bulletin of the Technical Committee on Data Engineering, IEEE Computer Society, Vol. 15, No. 1-4, 1992.

234. J. Widom, "The Starburst Active Database Rule System", IEEE Transactions on Knowledge and Data Engineering, Vol. 8, No. 4, Pp. 583-595, 1996.

235. B. Wu and K. Dube, "Applying Event-Condition-Action Mechanism in Healthcare: A Computerized Clinical Test-Ordering Protocol System (TOPS)", In IEEE 3rd International

Symposium on Cooperative Database Systems for Advanced Applications, Beijing, China, 2001.

236. B. Wu, E. Mansour, K. Dube and J. Li, "An Event-Driven Approach to Computerizing Clinical Guidelines Using XML", In Workshops on Proceedings of the IEEE Computing, 2006.

237. T. Xin and I. Ray, "Detection for conflicts of dependencies in advanced transaction models", In Proceedings of the 9th International Conference on Database Engineering and Application Symposium, Pp. 17-26, 2005.

238. T. Xin, Y. Zhu and I. Ray, "Reliable Scheduling of Advanced Transactions", Data and Applications Security XIX, Lecture Notes in Computer Science, Vol. 3654, Pp. 124-138, 2005.

239. D.S. Yadav, R. Agrawal, D.S. Chauhan, R.C. Saraswt and A.K. Majumdar, "Modeling Long Duration Transactions with Time Constraints in Active Database", In Proceedings of the International Conference on Information Technology: Coding and Computing Computer Society, Vol. 1, Pp. 497-501, 2004.

240. D.S. Yadav, R. Agrawal and R.C. Sarswat, "Analysis of Cooperation Semantics for Transaction Processing with Full and Partial Aborts in Active Database", In Proceedings of the 4th IEEE International Pacific Rim Conference on Multimedia, Information, Communication and Signal Processing, Singapore, ISBN:0-7803-8186-6, 2003.

241. C. Zaniolo, "Active Database Rules with Transaction-Conscious Stable-Model Semantics", In Proceedings of the 4th International Conference on Deductive and Object-Oriented Databases, Singapore, Pp. 55-72, 1995.

242. N. Zhang and T. Harder, "On Modeling Power of Object-Relational Data Models in Technical Applications", In Proceedings of the First East-European Symposium on Advances in Databases and Information Systems, St. Petersburg, Pp. 1-13, 1997.

243. N. Zhang, T. Harder and J. Thomas, "Enriching Object-Relational Databases with Relationship Semantics", In Proceedings of the 3rd International Workshop on Next Generation Information Technologies and Systems, Israel, Pp. 215-222, 1997.

244. W. Zhang and N. Ritter, "The real benefits of Object-Relational DB-Technology for Object-Oriented Software Development", In Proceedings of the 18th British National Conference on Databases, LNCS 2097, Springer, Pp. 89-104, 2001.

245. N. Zhang, N. Ritter and T. Harder, "Enriched Relationship Processing in Object-Relational Database Management Systems", In proceedings of the 3rd International Symposium on Cooperative Database Systems for Advanced Applications, Pp. 53-62, 2001.

246. G. Zhang, D. Deng, Z. Gong and Phillip C.Y Sheu, "Active Rule Processing Technology Application for Electronic Commerce", IEEE Computer Society, Pp. 389-393, 2009.

247. Q. Zheng and X. Bi, "An improved concurrency control algorithm for distributed real-time Database", In Proceedings of the IEEE International Conference on Advanced Management Science, Vol. 2, Pp. 364-367, 2010.

248. D. Zimmer and R. Unland, "On the semantics of complex events in active database management systems", In 15th International Conference on Proceedings of the Data Engineering, Pp. 392-399, 1999.

249. D. Zimmer, A. Meckenstock and R. Unland, "A General Model for Event Specification in Active Database Management Systems", In Proceedings of the 5th International Conference on Deductive and Object-Oriented Databases, Switzerland, Pp. 419-420, 1997.

250. P. Zong, J. Qin and Q. Yu, "Some Key Techniques in Active Information System", International Journal of Computer Science and Network Security, Vol. 7, No. 3, Pp. 21-26, 2007.